Aristop

Lysist.

The Focus Classical Library

Aristophanes: Acharnians • Jeffrey Henderson
Aristophanes: The Birds • Jeffrey Henderson
Aristophanes: Clouds • Jeffrey Henderson
Aristophanes: Frogs • Jeffrey Henderson
Aristophanes: Lysistrata • Jeffrey Henderson
Aristophanes: Three Comedies: Acharnians, Lysistrata, Clouds • Jeffrey Henderson
Euripides: The Bacchae • Stephen Esposito
Euripides: Four Plays: Medea, Hippolytus, Heracles, Bacchae • Stephen Esposito
Euripides: Hecuba • Robin Mitchell-Boyask
Euripides: Heracles • Michael R. Halleran
Euripides: Hippolytus • Michael R. Halleran
Euripides: Medea • Anthony Podlecki
Euripides: The Trojan Women • Diskin Clay
Golden Verses: Poetry of the Augustan Age • Paul T. Alessi
Golden Prose in the Age of Augustus • Paul T. Alessi
Hesiod: Theogony • Richard Caldwell
Hesiod: Theogony & Works and Days • Stephanie Nelson
The Homeric Hymns • Susan Shelmerdine
Ovid: Metamorphoses • Z. Philip Ambrose
Plautus: Captivi, Amphitryon, Casina, Pseudolus • David Christenson
Roman Comedy: Five Plays by Plautus and Terence • David Christenson
Roman Lives • Brian K. Harvey
Sophocles: Antigone • Ruby Blondell
Sophocles: Electra • Hanna M. Roisman
Sophocles: King Oidipous • Ruby Blondell
Sophocles: Oidipous at Colonus • Ruby Blondell
Sophocles: Philoktetes • Seth Schein
Sophocles: The Theban Plays • Ruby Blondell
Terence: Brothers (Adelphoe) • Charles Mercier
Vergil: The Aeneid • Richard Caldwell

Aristophanes
Lysistrata

Translated with
Introduction and Notes

Jeffrey Henderson
Boston University

Aristophanes
Lysistrata

© 1988 Jeffrey Henderson

Focus Publishing/R. Pullins Company
PO Box 369
Newburyport, MA 01950
www.pullins.com

Cover illustration © istockphoto/Jane Norton

ISBN 13: 978-0-941051-02-6
To see available eBook versions, visit www.pullins.com

Library of Congress 87-083734

Printed in the United States of America

18 17 16 15 14 13 12 11 10 9

0612V

For my parents,
Frank and Amy Henderson

Contents

Preface

Lysistrata, first performed in 411 BC, is, of all the plays of Aristophanes, probably the most popular with modern readers and audiences. Its lively and imaginative plot, its memorable heroine, its many good jokes, its appeal for peace and tolerance between the sexes and among people and nations give it a timeless appeal. Today it is just as entertaining as theater, and just as relevant as a view of the best and the worst of Western civilization, as it was over two millennia ago. In its mirror modern men and women can catch a glimpse of where we came from, where our best ideals have aimed us, and how far we have come (or not come) thus far.

This is a translation of *Lysistrata* into contemporary American verse, designed for both readers and performers, and presupposing no knowledge of classical Greece or classical Greek theater. I render the Greek text line by line so as to give a sense of its original scope and pace, using for the dialogue and songs verse-forms that are familiar to modern audiences. Where the original text refers to people, places, things and events whose significance modern audiences cannot reasonably be expected to comprehend, I have tried to find easily comprehensible alternatives that preserve the import of the original. The most important of these references are identified and discussed in the notes for the benefit of historically minded readers.

The conventions of Aristophanic comedy included the frank portrayal and discussion of religion, politics and sex (including nudity and obscenity). In *Lysistrata* all three are brilliantly intertwined. I have reproduced this feature as accurately as possible within my general guideline of easy comprehensibility. To do otherwise would be to falsify the play. These three areas are of fundamental importance to any society; one of Aristophanes' chief aims was to make humor of them while at the same time encouraging his audience to think about them in ways discouraged, or even forbid-

1

den, outside the comic theater. For those made uncomfortable by such a portrayal of one or more of these three areas of life, *Lysistrata* provides an opportunity to ask themselves why.

The Introduction contains sections on Aristophanes and the genre of Attic Old Comedy which his plays represent; *Lysistrata* and the historical situation to which it was originally addressed; conventions of ancient production with suggestions for modern performers; and suggestions for further reading. Like the translation and notes, the Introduction requires no previous expertise, and so is suitable for readers and students making their first acquaintance with Aristophanes.

The translation is based on my own edition of the Greek text, with Introduction and Commentary (Clarendon Press: Oxford 1987).

Los Angeles JJH
September 1987

MAP

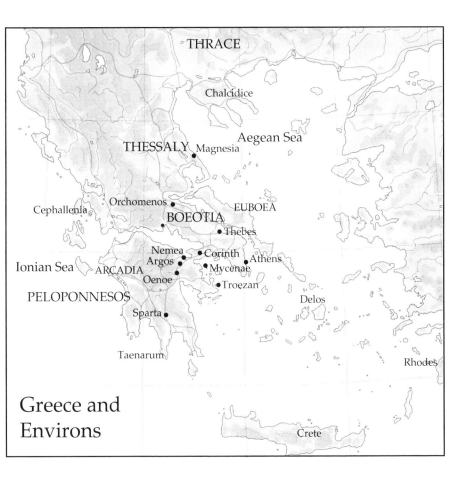

THRACE

Chalcidice

Aegean Sea

THESSALY Magnesia

Cephallenia

Orchomenos

BOEOTIA

EUBOEA

Thebes

Ionian Sea

Nemea

Corinth

Argos

Athens

ARCADIA

Mycenae

Oenoe

Troezan

PELOPONNESOS

Delos

Sparta

Taenarum

Rhodes

Greece and
Environs

Crete

Introduction

Aristophanes and Old Comedy

The period of Old Comedy at Athens began in 486 BC, when comedies first became part of the festival of the Greater Dionysia, and by convention ended in 388 BC, when Aristophanes produced his last play. During this period some 600 comedies were produced. We know the names of some fifty comic poets and the titles of some 300 plays. We have eleven complete plays by Aristophanes, the first one dating from 425, and several thousand fragments of other plays by Aristophanes and other poets, most of them only a line or so long and very few from plays written before 440.

The principal occasions for the production of comedies were the Greater Dionysia, held in March or April, and (from 440) the Lenaea, held in January or February. These were national festivals honoring the wine-god Dionysos (whose cult from very early times had included mimetic features), and the theatrical productions were competitions in which poets, dancers, actors, producers and musicians competed for prizes that were awarded by judges at the close of the festival. The Greater Dionysia was held in the Theater of Dionysos on the south slope of Acropolis and accommodated some 17,000 spectators, who included both Athenians and foreign visitors. The Lenaea, which only Athenians attended, was held elsewhere in the city (we do not know where). By the fourth century the Lenaea was held in the Theater of Dionysos also, but it is unclear when the relocation occurred.

At these festivals comedy shared the theater with tragedy and satyr-drama, which had been produced at the Greater Dionysia since the sixth century. The first contest in tragedy is dated to 534 (the poet Thespis is victorious), but it is not certain that this contest was held at the Greater Dionysia, and in any case this festival seems to have experienced major changes after the overthrow of the tyranny and the establishment of democracy, that is, after c. 508. Tragedy dramatized stories from heroic myth, emphasizing dire personal and social events that had befallen hero(in)es and their families in the distant past and mostly in places other than Athens. By convention, the poetry and music of tragedy were highly stylized and archaic. Satyr-drama, which was composed by the same poets who wrote tragedy, was the same, except that the heroic stories were treated in a humorous fashion and the chorus was composed of satyrs: mischievous followers of Dionysos who were part human and part animal.

Comedy, by contrast, had different conventions of performance (see III, below) and was also less restricted by conventions of language, music and subject. That is probably why the composers and performers of tragedy and satyr-drama were never the same ones who composed and performed comedy. The language of comedy was basically colloquial, though it often parodies the conventions of other (particularly tragic) poetry, and was free to include indecent, even obscene material. The music and dancing, too, tended to reflect popular styles. The favorite subjects of comedy were free-form mythological burlesque; domestic situations featuring everyday character types; and political satire portraying people and events of current interest in the public life of the Athenians. Our eleven surviving comedies all fall into this last category. Mythological and domestic comedy contin-ued to flourish after the Old Comic period, but political comedy seems to have died out: a casualty of social and political changes following the Athenians' loss of the Peloponnesian War, and with it their empire, in 404. To understand the significance of political comedy, we must first look at the political system of which it was an organic feature: the phase of radical democracy inaugurated by the reforms of Ephialtes in 462/1 and lasting until the end of the century.

Democracy means 'rule of the demos' (sovereign people). In fifth-cen-tury Athens democracy was radical in that the sovereignty of the demos was more absolute than in any other society before or since. The demos consisted of all citizen males at least eighteen years of age. All decisions affecting the governance and welfare of the state were made by the direct and unappealable vote of the demos. The state was managed by members of the demos at least thirty years of age who were chosen by lot and who held office in periods ranging from one day to one year. The only excep-tions were military commanders, who were elected to one-year terms, and holders of certain ancient priesthoods, who inherited their positions. The demos determined by vote whether or not anyone holding any public posi-tion was qualified to do his job and, after completion of his term, whether he had done it satisfactorily. All military commanders, and most holders of powerful allotted offices, came from the wealthy classes, but their success depended on the good will of the demos as a whole.

One of the most important allotted offices was that of choregos (sponsor of a chorus). Choregoi were allotted from a list of men wealthy enough to hold this office, for they had to recruit and pay for the training, costuming, and room and board of the chorus that would perform at one of the festivals. In the case of a comic chorus this involved 24 dancers and the musicians who would accompany them. Being choregos gave a man an opportunity to display his wealth and refinement for the benefit of the demos as a whole and to win a prize that would confer prestige on himself and his dancers. Some wealthy men therefore volunteered to be choregoi instead of waiting for their names to be drawn. On the other hand, a man who put on a cheap or otherwise unsatisfactory chorus could expect to suffer a significant loss of public prestige.

All other expenses, including stipends for the poet and his actors and for prizes, were undertaken by vote of the demos and paid from public funds. A poet got a place in the festival by submitting a draft some six months in advance to the office-holder in charge of the festival. Ancient sources say that at least the choral parts of the proposed play had to be submitted. How much more was submitted we do not know. But revision up to the day of the performance was certainly possible, since many allusions in comedy refer to events occurring very shortly before the festival: most notably the death of Sophocles shortly before the performance of *Frogs* in 405.

If he got on the program, the poet would be given his stipend and assigned his actors. He and the choregoi would then set about getting the performance ready for the big day, the poet acting as music director, choreographer and director, the choregoi rounding up, and paying the expenses of, the best dancers he could find. Tragic poets produced three tragedies and a satyr-drama, comic poets one comedy.

Thus comedy, as a theatrical spectacle, was an organic feature of the Athenian democracy. But its poetic, musical and mimetic traditions were much older, deriving from forms of entertainment developed by cultivated members of the aristocratic families that had governed Attica before the democracy. One such form was the komos (band of revellers), which gave comedy (komoidia: 'song of the komos') its name. A komos was made up of some solidary group (a military, religious or family group, for example), often in disguise, which entertained onlookers on many kinds of festive and religious occasions.

Part of the entertainment was abuse and criticism of individuals or groups standing outside the solidarity of the komos. The victims might be among the onlookers or they might be members of a rival komos. The komos sang and danced as a group, and its leader (who was no doubt also the poet) could speak by himself to his komos, to the onlookers or to a rival komos-leader. No doubt at a very early stage komos was a competitive entertainment by which a given group could, in artistic ways, make those claims and criticisms against rival groups which at other times they might make in more overtly political ways.

Aside from its value as entertainment, the tradition of the komos was useful in allowing the expression of personal and political hostilities which would otherwise have been difficult to express safely: the misbehavior of powerful individuals, disruptive but unactionable gossip, the shortcomings of citizens in groups or as a whole. In this capacity komos served as a social safety valve, allowing a relatively harmless airing of tensions before they could become dangerous, and also as a means of social communication and social control, upholding generally held norms and calling attention to derelictions.

But in addition to its critical and satirical aspects, komos had, like all festive activities, an idealistic side, envisaging the community as it would be if everyone agreed on the norms and lived up to them, and a utopian side as well, imagining how wonderful life would be if reality were as human beings would like it to be. In this capacity komos provided a welcome relief from the cares and burdens of everyday life.

Old Comedies were theatrical versions of komos: the band of dancers with their leader was now a comic chorus involved in a story enacted by actors on a stage. The chorus still resembled a komos in two ways. As performers, it competed against rival choruses, and in its dramatic identity it initially represented a distinct group or groups: in *Lysistrata*, for example, it consists of lower-class old men who are hostile to the heroine versus upper-class old women who support her. The comic chorus differs from a komos in that at a certain point in the play it drops its special identity and thereafter represents the celebrating community (spectators) as a whole. At this point, its leader often steps forward, on behalf of the poet, to advise and admonish the spectators, and his chorus might sing abusive songs about individuals in the audience.

The actors in the stage-area had been amalgamated with the chorus during the sixth century. Their characteristic costumes (III, below) and antics were depicted in vase-paintings of this period in many parts of Greece, suggesting a much older tradition of comic mimesis. As early as the Homeric period (8th and 7th centuries) we find mythological burlesque and such proto-comedy as the Thersites-episode in the second book of the Iliad. In this period, too, the iambic poets flourished. Named for the characteristic rhythm of their verses, which also became the characteristic rhythm of actors in Athenian drama, the iambic poets specialized in self-revelation, popular story-telling, earthy gossip, and personal enmities, often impersonating someone else or creating fictitious first-person identities. They were credited with pioneering poetic styles of invective, obscenity and colloquialism.

The characters on the Old Comic stage preserved many of these traditions, but like the chorus they were an adaptation to the democratic festivals, most notably in political comedy. In Aristophanes' plays, the world depicted by the plot and the characters on stage was the world of the spectators in their civic roles: as heads of families and participants in governing the state. We see the demos in its various capacities; the competitors for public influence; the men who hold or seek offices; the social, artistic and intellectual celebrities. We hear formal debate on current issues, including its characteristic invective. We get a decision, complete with winners and losers, and we see the outcome. This depiction of public life was designed both to arouse laughter and to encourage reflection about people and events in ways not possible in other public contexts. Thus it was at once a distorted and an accurate depiction of public life, like a modern political cartoon.

The characters fall into two main categories: sympathetic and unsympathetic. The sympathetic ones, like Lysistrata, are fictitious creations embodying ideal civic types. The unsympathetic ones, like the Magistrate, embody disapproved civic behavior and usually represent specific leaders or categories of leaders. The sympathetic characters advocate positions held by political minorities and are therefore 'outsiders'. But they are shown winning out against the unsympathetic ones, who represent the current status quo. Characters or chorus-members representing the demos as a whole are portrayed as initially sceptical or hostile to the sympathetic characters, but in the end are persuaded. Thus the comic poets tried to persuade the actual demos (the spectators) to change its mind about issues that had been decided but might be changed. Aristophanes at least once succeeded: after the performance of *Frogs* he was awarded a crown by the city for the advice given by the chorus-leader in that play.

In this way, the institution of Old Comedy performed functions essential to any democracy: public airing of minority views and open criticism of those holding power. In this function, the Old Comic festivals were organized protest. But they were also an opportunity to articulate civic ideals: one identified the shortcomings of the status quo by holding it up against a vision of things as they ought to be. The use of satire and criticism within a utopian plot addressing itself to important issues of national scope was thus a democratic adaptation of such pre-democratic traditions as komos and iambic poetry. That the comic festivals were state-run and not privately organized is striking evidence of the openness and self-confidence of a full democracy: the demos was completely in charge, so it did not fear attacks on its leaders or resent admonition by the poets.

The comic poets did not, however, enjoy complete license to say anything they pleased. Were that the case they could not have expected anyone to take what they had to say seriously. Following each festival there was an assembly in which anyone who had a legal complaint could come forward. Like any other public voices, comic poets had to avoid slander (malicious and unfounded abuse) and could not criticize the democratic constitution and the inherent rightness of the demos' rule. Nor could they speak ill of the dead or compromise the integrity of the state religion. If the criticism and abuse we find in Old Comedy often seems outrageous by our standards, it is because we differ from fifth-century Athenians in our definition of outrageous, not because comic poets were held to no standards.

Aristophanes, for example, was twice sued by the politician Cleon, once for slandering the demos in front of visiting foreigners (in the lost play *Babylonians*) and once for slandering him (in *Knights*). In the first instance the demos decided not to hear the case. In the second the poet and the politician settled out of court (Aristophanes subsequently boasted that he had not abided by the settlement). The demos could also enact new laws restricting comic freedoms. One of these was enacted in 415 and forbade mention by name in comedy of any of the men who had recently been prosecuted for parodying the Eleusinian Mysteries of Demeter. Evidently the demos wanted these men to be officially forgotten and perhaps feared that mention of their names might pollute the festival. In addition, the demos did not want to take the chance that a comic poet might speak sympathetically of them as they often spoke for other underdogs.

With these general characteristics of Old Comedy in mind, let us now turn to *Lysistrata* and its contribution to public entertainment and political debate in the winter of 411 BC.

Lysistrata, and the Events of 411

An Athenian woman named Lysistrata ('Disbander of Armies') organizes and successfully prosecutes a panhellenic conspiracy of citizen wives that forces the chief combatants (Athens and Sparta) and their allies to negotiate a peaceful settlement of the war and promise never again to fight one another. Her conspiracy consists of two plots. One is a conjugal strike staged by young wives from the warring cities and designed to force their warrior-husbands to lay down their arms and come home. The other is the occupation of the Athenian citadel (Acropolis) and its treasuries by the older wives of Athens, so that the politicians will no longer be able to finance the war. The strike-plot (described in the prologue and illustrated at 706-13) succeeds virtually unopposed. The occupation-plot (254-705) contains the agonistic component of the play: strife between choruses of old men and old women, and a contest between Lysistrata and an old Magistrate. When the occupation-plot has eliminated official opposition, and the strike-plot has made the husbands capitulate to their wives, Athenian and Spartan Ambassadors negotiate their differences and promise eternal friendship.

The plot of *Lysistrata* is characteristic of Aristophanes' heroic plays (the others are *Acharnians*, *Peace*, *Birds* and *Assemblywomen*). By means of a fantastic scheme a hero(ine), who represents a class of citizens who feel frustrated or victimized by the operations of contemporary society, manages to evade or alter the situation of which (s)he initially complains and proceeds to effect a triumph of wish-fulfillment over reality. Those powers human, natural or divine which would obstruct the scheme are either converted by argument or overcome by guile, magic or force. At the end there is a restoration of normality (typically portrayed in terms of an idealized civic past) and a celebration in which only the hero(ine)'s supporters participate, for the obstructors and those who would undeservedly benefit by the hero(ine)'s success have been expelled.

Although the hero(ine) typically represents the views of a social and political minority, and the scheme bypasses or undermines the powers currently enforcing the status quo, the hero(ine)'s goal is one likely to be shared by most spectators and the argument (s)he uses to defend it appeal to their interests and sense of justice. The powers are portrayed entirely unsympathetically as self-interested, corrupt and misguided, and the status quo as burdensome for ordinary, decent people and as quite unnecessary. In *Lysistrata*, the politicians (represented by the Magistrate) are portrayed as prosecuting the war to make a profit at the expense of the demos and its fighting men. Their claim that there is no alternative to war is shown to be false: love (or, more precisely, sex) can conquer all. Once the Magistrate is discredited and eliminated, the Men's Chorus (representing the demos) and the Ambassadors (representing the warriors) agree to reconcile their feud and live happily ever after.

In this utopian scenario, the harsh and intractable realities of life, politics and international aggression are transformed so that wives manage to overcome husbands, insignificant citizens manage to discredit powerful ones, Athens obtains a peace that allows her to keep her empire intact, and the Spartans turn out to be jolly good fellows after all. The transformation seems quite plausible because Aristophanes appeals to the wishes of the spectators for a better world, the world as it presumably was in the good old days before the war, where all would be happy and prosperous and where there would be no more violence. He also appeals to the feeling of average citizens that their wishes would be more likely to come true were there no authorities in the way, constantly reminding them of unpleasant duties. This combination of regressive wish-fulfillment and oedipal rebellion allows a communal release of tensions. Insofar as their release is motivated by acceptable civic ideals (peace and solidarity) and achieved in humorous fantasy (wives determining policy), it was safe, cohesive not divisive. But insofar as it was a valid expression of people's real war-weariness, an expression of social currents running beneath the surface of public discourse, it was also fair warning to the demos' leaders that public patience might not last indefinitely.

The Peloponnesian War between Athens and her island empire and Sparta and her allies had begun in 431 after several decades of tension. Sparta and Athens had emerged from the Persian Wars fifty years earlier as the two superpowers of Greece. Relying on her navy, Athens had turned a defensive island alliance against Persia into a tribute-paying empire composed of small subject states with democratic governments controlled by the Athenian demos. Sparta, the chief city of the Peloponnesus (lower half of mainland Greece) and the greatest land power in Greece, feared the growing power of this empire and also the spread of 'tyrannical' democracy.

From the outset a significant minority at Athens resisted the war. These were the inhabitants of the Attic countryside: farmers who had little to gain from the war and many of whom were of the landed aristocracy. The war-plan, which granted Sparta supremacy on land, required that these citizens abandon their ancestral estates to the invaders and move into the city for the duration of the war. Athens initially expected a quick victory, but only after ten years of indecisive warfare was the peace of Nicias arranged in 421. The peace proved to be only a time-out, lasting only until 418, when Athens accused Sparta of violating its terms.

The war had begun to go decisively against Athens in 413, when their great expedition to Sicily, launched in 415, was wiped out at Syracuse, with crippling losses of men, material and wealth. By the end of 412, Athens had somehow managed to stave off defeat by winning back some strategic territory and rebuilding an effective navy. The political and fiscal discipline required to do this was facilitated by the appointment of an extraordinary board of ten elderly statesmen who could expedite the war-effort by by-passing the demos assembly. One of these magistrates is the heroine's antagonist in *Lysistrata*. Nevertheless, at the time of *Lysistrata* (January or February 411), the city of Athens was still surrounded by a Spartan army of occupation; many of her subject allies had revolted; all her remaining wealth had been used to rebuild the navy; her leadership was dangerously divided; and anti-democratic groups were busy undermining popular faith in the leadership and even in the democratic constitution. It was clear that getting acceptable terms in negotiation with the Peloponnesians was out of the question unless significant victories were forthcoming.

The audience that watched *Lysistrata* did not yet know that the officers of the main Athenian naval base at Samos had suspended the democratic constitution, entered into secret negotiations with Persia for financial aid, and were negotiating with the exiled aristocrat Alcibiades, who wanted to return to Athens on condition that the constitution were changed in such a way that his democratic enemies would lose power. The general, Pisander, whom Lysistrata calls a thief, had recently returned from Samos to engineer these changes. The following months saw a right-wing terror campaign at Athens, using assassination and intimidation, and by summer the democracy had been replaced by an oligarchic government.

Aristophanes has always opposed the war: conflict between Athens and Sparta weakened Greece and conflict between Athenians weakened the democracy. In his plays he argued for peaceful relations among Greeks and for civic solidarity at home, and he attacked the motives of the pro-war urban majority. In the 420's his anti-war heroes had been relocated Athenian countrymen. In 411 the hero was female. As far as we know, this was a novel idea in political comedy. Tragedy, which dealt with heroic families, had long had heroines, but political comedy portrayed public life, where citizen women were invisible. To understand Aristophanes' surprising choice we must look at *Lysistrata*'s real-life counterparts.

In democratic Athens the roles of women and men were mutually exclusive and mutually defining, with no overlap. Women managed the private world of the household and its finances, while men managed the public world of the city. Thus women had no opportunity to voice an opinion publicly on any matter and were in fact, as far as practicable, secluded from public view. The primary reason for this division of roles and seclusion of citizen women was that citizenship depended upon being unquestionably the child of a citizen father and mother, so that one's bride had to be demonstrably virginal and one's wife had to be demonstrably faithful. Not surprisingly, wives were stereotypically frivolous, naive, weak and untrustworthy: creatures who required protective seclusion.

In *Lysistrata* Aristophanes reverses these roles. The world of the household and its female managers becomes dominant over the men's public world. Wives use their traditional domestic weapons (complaint, dereliction of duties and passive resistance) in a corporate conspiracy designed to influence the men's public sphere: they exclude men from the domestic sphere just as men had excluded them from the public sphere. The older women, who had greater freedom of movement owing to their being past childbearing age, forcibly seize and occupy the state treasuries, which are assimilated to the family coffers of an individual household. The women argue that, as mothers, they have a stake in the war equal to the men's, and as household managers they have just as much skill, and more prudence, than do male political managers. Since the men have failed to win the war, it is time for the women to offer advice about how to end it. In the showdown, the husbands choose the security and happiness of wife and household over the danger and hardships of war. The world returns to normality.

The idea of women as saviors appealed to Aristophanes not only because of its brilliant novelty but also because it solved some difficult problems confronting a poet with an anti-war message in early 411. The volatile political atmosphere discouraged the usual finger-pointing, and an appeal for solidarity ruled out any portrayal of embattled political factions, such as the farmer-versus-urbanite scenario of the 420's. Somehow Aristophanes had to find respectable citizens who could make plausible arguments for reconciliation at home and abroad while at the same time standing outside and above the prevailing political turmoil and the military uncertainty. Women were his solution. They had a vested interest in the war and had sacrificed much; they represented every age-group and social class; they were integral to the city and yet stood outside its politics; and they had had nothing to do with bringing on the war in the first place. Through his women, Aristophanes could rebuke and advise the Athenians without appearing to be partisan, and in case the spectators should be offended they would have to admit that it was only women talking.

The heroine is nevertheless extraordinary. She is identified neither as a housewife nor as elderly. In the strike and in the seizure of the citadel she is the strategist and spokesman, while the other women are her agents. She understands and uses her helpers' talents but does not herself share in them, pointedly differentiating herself especially from the young wives. Moreover, she represents not only her own sex and city but advocates traditional values for all Greeks, male and female. She is endowed with an intelligence and will that would be extraordinary in a citizen of either sex and that triumphs on all fronts. In her possession of the most admired attributes, in her dual role as defender of home and of city, in her acquaintance with both domestic and martial arts, in her panhellenic outlook, in her advocacy of internal solidarity, in her cool discipline and immunity to sexual temptation, in her appeal to young and old and in her close connection to the citadel, Lysistrata, finds her closest analogue in the Athenian city-goddess Athena herself, whose temples were on the Acropolis and symbolized every individual household.

This analogy was facilitated by Lysistrata's resemblance to the most prominent woman in Athens, the priestess of Athena Polias, who in 411 was a woman who bore the virtually identical name Lysimache. Like all Polias priestesses, Lysimache came from the ancient family of the Eteobutadae, for this priesthood was immemorially older than the democracy and represented the most venerable traditions of Athens. Lysimache held office for sixty-four years and appears to have been publicly known, or thought, to be opposed to the war. By assimilating his heroine to such an august person, Aristophanes invested her with the maximum possible respectability. As always, Aristophanes uses the language of democracy to criticize the democracy's policies. Anyone who attacks majority views is wise to wrap himself in the flag.

Aristophanes was also careful in his choice of Lysistrata's opponents, who must represent the majority view and also be portrayed unsympathetically. Here Aristophanes makes different choices than in earlier plays, avoiding active politicians and military commanders. The unnamed Magistrate was a bureaucrat and functionary recently drawn out of retirement, a member of an emergency board that had usurped some of the demos' functions. His comic mistreatment was unlikely to arouse much spectator indignation. The old men of the chorus are irascible bores who earn a miserable living at the city's expense by serving on jury-courts, but who nevertheless behave arrogantly. The young Athenian warriors and ambassadors are caricatured gently, their only weakness being sexual desperation for their wives. Their Spartan counterparts are unmistakably weaker and more eager for peace, and they are easily outbargained in the negotiations.

Thus Aristophanes managed to carry out the aims of political comedy—humorous and reassuring fantasy that made a serious appeal—even on the subject of a war that might well be disastrously lost, and even in the explosive atmosphere of early 411.

Production

Since fifth-century comic poets put on a play for a particular competition and did not envisage future productions, an original script that later circulated as a text for readers contained only the words, with few if any attributions of lines to speakers and no stage directions. These had to be inferred from the text itself, so that all editions and translations, ancient and modern, differ to some extent in reconstructing the theatricality of the text. This means that anyone reading or performing an ancient comedy has a perfect right to bring the text to life in any way that seems appropriate: we have no information about how lines were originally distributed or performed and no idea of the original action on stage or in the orchestra. Thus there can be no 'authentic' production of an ancient comedy.

In this translation I assign speakers who seem to be the likeliest candidates for given lines: the reader is free to differ. I do not, however, supply stage-directions. One of the pleasures of reading or performing an ancient comedy is imagining how it might be realized in action. I hesitate to put my own imagination in the way of the reader's or producer's. This script is like a keyboard score by Bach, containing only the notes and leaving instruments and style up to the performer. In the end it is pointless to argue which performed version is 'authentic': only satisfied spectators really count.

We do know some facts about fifth-century comic theater, however, and there is no harm in reviewing them for their historical interest.

The actors wore masks, made of cork or papier mache, that covered the entire head. These were usually generic (young man, old woman, etc.) but might occasionally be special, like a portrait-mask of a prominent citizen. Their clothing was contemporary except that, whenever possible, it accommodated the traditional comic features of big stomach and rump and (for men) the phallos, made of leather and either dangling or (as in *Lysistrata*) erect. All roles were played by men. The naked women who often appear were men wearing body-stockings to which breasts and genitalia were attached. The city supplied an equal number of actors to each competing poet, probably three, and these actors played all the speaking roles. In *Birds*, for example, there are 22 speaking roles, but the script's exits and entrances are so arranged that three actors can play them all. Some plays, like *Lysistrata*, require a fourth or fifth actor. Perhaps in given years the allotment changed, or novices were periodically allowed to take smaller roles, or the poet could add extra actors at his own expense.

In the orchestra was a chorus of 24 men who sang and danced to the accompaniment of an aulos, a wind instrument that had two recorder-like pipes played simultaneously by a specially costumed player; and there could be other instruments as well. Like actors, members of the chorus wore masks and costumes appropriate to their identity. There could be dialogue between the chorus-leader and actors on stage, but the chorus as a whole only sings and dances. There was no ancient counterpart to the 'choral speaking' often heard in modern performances of Greek drama. The choral songs of comedy were in music and language usually in a popular style, and the dancing was expressive, adding a visual dimension to the words.

The stage-area was a slightly raised platform behind the large orchestra. Behind it was a wooden two-story building called the skene ('tent'), with two or three doors at stage-level, windows at the second story, and a roof on which actors could appear. On the roof was a crane called the mechane ('machine'), on which performers could fly above the stage (as gods, for example, whence the term *deus ex machina*). Another piece of permanent equipment was a wheeled platform called the ekkyklema, on which actors and scenery could be wheeled onstage to 'reveal' interior action. A painted or otherwise decorated plywood facade could be attached to the building if a particular play required it, and movable props and other scenery were used as needed. Since plays were performed in a large outdoor amphitheater, all entrances and exits of performers and objects took place in full view of the spectators. All in all, more demand was made on the spectators' imagination than in modern illusionistic theater, so that the performers must often tell the spectators what they are supposed to see.

A fifth-century comedy was played through without intermissions, the performance taking about two hours. The usual structure was a prologue (actors); the entry, called the parodos, of the chorus (chorus); a contest, called the agon (actors and chorus); the self-proclamation, or parabasis, of the chorus and its leader (chorus); and a series of episodes (actors) articulated by choral songs. In this translation I have supplied appropriate act-divisions, but performers should, as always, feel free to arrange their own performance as they see fit.

This translation is designed to be perfectly comprehensible to contemporary readers, and the best way to stage it is to make it just as comprehensible to the audience for whom one expects to perform it, using whatever human and other resources are available. Balloons, for example, make perfectly good phalloi, and music for the songs and moves for the dancers can be as simple or as elaborate as one cares to make them. Adaptations of characters, and insertion of allusions, to current events make for liveliness. The battle of the sexes seems always relevant and needs very little adaptation. But the political battle does: the Magistrate, for example, might represent any current government 'warmonger', the semichorus of old men might be any super-patriots, such as the veterans of World War II; the Spartans may be Soviets; and so forth.

This play has proven its stageworthiness; the best guide for performance is the text itself.

General Bibliography

Ancient sources for the production of classical drama are collected and discussed in the following.

Csapo, E. and Slater, W.J. *The Context of Ancient Drama* (Ann Arbor 1995)

Green, J.R. *Theatre in Ancient Greek Society* (London and New York 1994)

Pickard-Cambridge, A.W. *Dithyramb, Tragedy and Comedy*, rev. by T.B.L. Webster (Oxford 1962)

_____ *The Dramatic Festivals of Athens*, rev. by J. Gould and D.M. Lewis (Oxford 1968, rev. 1988)

Taplin, O. *Comic Angels and Other Approaches to Greek Drama through Vase-Paintings* (Oxford 1993)

Walcot, P. *Greek Drama in its Theatrical and Social Context* (Cardiff 1976)

Webster, T.B.L. *Greek Theatre Production* (London 1970)

Good general treatments of Aristophanic comedy are:

Arnott, P. *Greek Scenic Conventions in the Fifth Century B.C.* (Oxford 1962)

Bowie, A.M. *Aristophanes. Myth, Ritual and Comedy* (Cambridge 1993)

Cartledge, P. *Aristophanes and his Theatre of the Absurd* (London 1990)

Dover, K.J. *Aristophanic Comedy* (California 1972)

Harriott, R.M. *Aristophanes, Poet and Dramatist* (Baltimore 1986)

Hubbard, T.K. *The Mask of Comedy. Aristophanes and the Intertextual Parabasis* (Ithaca 1991)

MacDowell, D.M. *Aristophanes and Athens* (Oxford 1995)

McLeish, K. *The Theatre of Aristophanes* (New York 1980)

Moulton, C. *Aristophanic Poetry* (Hypomnemata 68: Göttingen 1981)

Reckford, K.J. *Aristophanes' Old-and-New Poetry* (Chapel Hill 1987)

Russo, C.F. *Aristophanes, an Author for the Stage* (London 1994)

Sifakis, G. *Parabasis and Animal Choruses* (London 1971)

Sommerstein, A.H. et al., eds. *Tragedy, Comedy and the Polis* (Bari 1993)

Stone, L.M. *Costume in Aristophanic Comedy* (New York 1981)

Whitman, C.H. *Aristophanes and the Comic Hero* (Cambridge MA 1964)

Winkler, J.J. and Zeitlin, F.I., eds. *Nothing to Do With Dionysos? Athenian Drama in its Social Context* (Princeton 1990)

Suggestions for Further Reading

Readers interested in the Greek text are referred to my edition (see Preface).

Ancient information about comedy is collected by A.W. Pickard-Cambridge in *Dithyramb, Tragedy and Comedy*, rev. by T.B.L. Webster (Oxford 1962), and about the theatrical festivals in the same author's *The Dramatic Festivals of Athens*, rev. by J. Gould and D.M. Lewis (Oxford 1968).

Recent studies on *Lysistrata* include:

Dillon, M. "The *Lysistrata* as a Post-Decelean Peace Play," *Transactions of the American Philological Association* 117 (1987) 97-104

Foley, H. P. "The 'Female Intruder' Reconsidered: Women in Aristophanes' *Lysistrata* and *Ecclesiazasue*," *Classical Philology* 77 (1982) 1-21

Harriot, R. M. "*Lysistrata*: Action and Theme," in J. Redmond, ed. *Themes in Drama Vll: Drama, Sex and Politics (Cambridge* 1985) 11-22

Henderson, J. "Older Women in Attic Old Comedy," *Transactions of the American Philological Association* 117 (1987) 105-29

Vaio, J. "The Manipulation of Theme and Action in Aristophanes' *Lysistrata*," *Greek Roman and Byzantine Studies* 14 (1973) 369-80

Westlake, H. D. "The *Lysistrata* and the War," *Phoenix* 34 (1980) 38-54

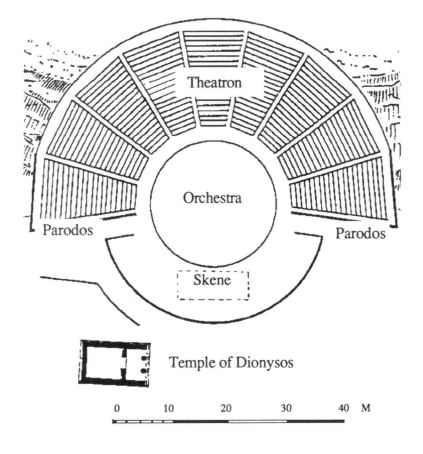

A reconstruction of the
Theater of Dionysos in Athens

Aristophanes' *Lysistrata*

CHARACTERS

SPEAKING CHARACTERS

Lysistrata, an Athenian woman
Calonice, an Athenian wife
Myrrhine, an Athenian wife
Lampito, a Spartan woman
Magistrate, an Athenian bureaucrat
Old Women, three helpers of Lysistrata

Rod, Myrrhine's husband
Spartan Herald
Spartan Ambassador
Athenian Ambassador
Athenian, friend of the
    Ambassador

MUTE CHARACTERS

Athenian Wives
Foreign Wives
Policewoman with Wives
Slaves with Magistrate
Police with Magistrate
Athenian Old Women

Nurse with Rod
Baby with Rod
Reconciliation, a naked girl
Spartan Husbands
Athenian Husbands
Doorkeeper

CHORUS

Old War-Veterans, twelve

Old Wives, twelve

SCENE I

Lysistrata

If I'd invited them to drink some wine°
or talk about the kids or go out dancing,
you'd hear the sound of high heels everywhere.
But now there's not a single wife in sight.

---

1   Comic wives are conventionally portrayed as very fond of drinking, dancing and noise-making. In reality, wives' everyday access to wine and opportunities for revelry were severely restricted by husbands. But at some festivals (those honoring the wine-god Dionysus, for example) these restrictions were relaxed, and at others (those exclusive to women) they were unenforceable. Women could also meet together informally at a shrine: here Lysistrata mentions shrines of Dionysus, Pan and Aphrodite. Comedians, who catered to male audiences, portrayed wives' religious activities as mere excuses for drinking and revelry. Aristophanes exploits this stereotype extensively in his portrayal of the wives in this play, but from the start he is careful to exempt the heroine.

Well, here's my next-door neighbor, anyway.   5
Hi, Calonice.°

Calonice
    Hi to you, Lysistrata.
Hey, why the dirty looks? Cheer up, kiddo.
Don't frown, you'll wrinkle up your pretty face.

Lysistrata
I'm angry, Calonice, deeply hurt,
in fact offended by the wives, by *us*,   10
because, according to our husbands we're
the best at clever schemes—

Calonice
        And that's the truth.

Lysistrata
—but when I tell them all to meet me here,
to scheme about the most important things,
they're sleeping in and don't show up.

Calonice
        They'll show.   15
It's not so easy getting out this early.
We've got to do our husbands little favors,
we've got to get the servants out of bed,
we've got to wash and feed and burp the kids.

Lysistrata
But they've got more important things to do   20
than those!

Calonice
    OK, Lysistrata, suppose
you tell me why we're meeting here. The deal.
Is it a big one?

Lysistrata
    Very big.

Calonice
        Not hard as well?

Lysistrata
It's very hard.

---

6 In Greek the name Calonice means 'Fair Victory' ('Victoria' would be a modern equivalent),
but it is an untypical form of the name and so may have been specially chosen: to suggest an
upper-class background, or perhaps even to allude to an actual person.

Calonice
    Then why aren't we all here?°

Lysistrata
    No, no, not that: if it were that, they'd come.   25
    It's something I've been thinking hard *about*:
    on sleepless nights I've tossed it back and forth.

Calonice
    I guess it must be pretty limp by now.

Lysistrata
    It's limp all right! So limp that the salvation
    of all of Greece lies in the women's hands!   30

Calonice
    In women's hands? We're goners then for sure!

Lysistrata
    The nation's fate is in our hands alone!
    The very existence of the Spartan people—

Calonice
    It's best they *don't* exist, in my opinion.

Lysistrata
    and all of Thebes completely obliterated—   35

Calonice
    Not all of Thebes: please save the caviar!°

Lysistrata
    and I don't even want to mention Athens:
    You know what I could say: you fill it in.
    But all the women, if they'd only come,
    the Theban women and the Spartan women   40
    and us, together we could rescue Greece!

Calonice
    But what can women do that's sensible,
    or grand? We're good at putting make-up on,
    designer clothes and wigs and necklaces,
    imported gowns and fancy lingerie!   45

---

24   In addition to fondness for drink (1 n.) ungovernable sexual appetite was another stereotype of wives that Aristophanes fully exploits. By contrast, men were conventionally supposed to be able to discipline their appetites. A main source of humor in this play was the reversal of these gender roles: the women resist sexual temptation while the men succumb.

36   Thebes was the main city of Boeotia, which exported fine eels, a luxury item now contraband in Athens because Thebes was a major enemy. Aristophanes reminds the audience of such war-time deprivations (see 700 ff.).

Lysistrata

And that's exactly what will save us all:
the little gowns, the perfumes, and the slippers,
the make-up and the see-through lingerie!

Calonice

And how do you figure that?

Lysistrata

        No man alive
will want to lift his spear against another—   50

Calonice

I guess I better go and buy some clothes!

Lysistrata

or lift his shield—

Calonice

        I'll put my best dress on!

Lysistrata

or draw his sword.

Calonice

        I've got to buy some slippers.

Lysistrata

So don't you think the women should have come?

Calonice

Have come? They should have taken wings and flown!   55

Lysistrata

But look around, our fellow Athenians
are late as always, chronically delayed.
But I'd have thought the women from the beach towns
and the islands—

Calonice

        Lighten up, I know they're coming:
the island girls are good at riding topside.   60

Lysistrata

But what about the women from that town°
that's always being burnt? I thought that they
would be the first.

Calonice

        That shipping magnate's wife,

---

61   The residents of Acharnae, whose land was especially hard hit during the war and who were therefore especially eager to punish the Spartans. They were the chorus of Aristophanes' peace-play *Acharnians*, produced in 425.

at any rate, is coming: she packed her schooner.°   65
But look, I see some women coming now!

Lysistrata
And there's another bunch!

Calonice
        But what's that smell?
What's *their* town?

Lysistrata
        Garlicville.

Calonice
        I might have guessed:
they must have walked right through it on their way.

Myrrhine°
I hope we're not too late, Lysistrata.
Well. What's the matter?

Lysistrata
        I'm upset, Myrrhine,   70
when a woman's late for such important meetings.

Myrrhine
I couldn't find my girdle: it was dark.
But now we're here: so tell us what's important!

Lysistrata
Let's cool our heels a little while longer,
until the Thebans and the Spartans have a chance   75
to get here.

Myrrhine
        Sure, let's wait, you're running things.
Hey, hold it, here's the Spartan Lampito!°

---

65   schooner (boat and large drinking glass) makes fun of women's fondness for alcohol and teases Theogenes, who apparently had lost a merchant ship the previous year.

69   Myrrhine (meaning 'myrtle') was a very common woman's name, but was chosen in this play because it also was a Greek slang term for the female genitals: 'Pussy' is a good modern equivalent. Myrrhine represents the typical young wife, a category that, in Athenian terms, primarily signified sexuality.

77   The name Lampito is typically Spartan. In this play all the Spartans speak a thick, caricatured version of their local dialect, Laconian from Laconia, the region in southern (Peloponnesian) Greece where Sparta is located; Athenians spoke the Attic dialect of their own region, Attica. Although Attic and Laconian are both dialects of Greek, they differed substantially. Athenians and Spartans were not only different in culture and government but also considered themselves racially different, Athenians being Ionian and Spartans Dorian. Translators and performers are free to choose an appropriate modern dialect.

Lysistrata
Lampito, darling, greetings from us all.
What a gorgeous specimen, you lovely thing!
What healthy skin, what firmness of physique!   80
You could take on a bull!

Lampito
                              Is not impossible.
I go to gym, I make my buttocks hard.

Calonice
I've never seen a pair of boobs like that!

Lampito
You feel them: like blue-ribbon ox, you think!

Lysistrata
And this young lady here, where's she come from?   85

Lampito
Distinguished comrade from collective farm
of Thebes.

Myrrhine
        I knew she had to be from Thebes:
she looks so natural and organic.

Calonice
                                Yes,
her organs have a cultivated look.

Lysistrata
And who is this one?

Lampito
                      Representative   90
from Gulf.°

Calonice
            She's got some pretty gulfs herself.
Here's one in front, and here's another one.

Lampito
Well: who convenes this revolutionary cell
of women?

Lysistrata
          I did.

Lampito
                Please to tell us then
agenda of the meeting.

---

91   Corinth, on the Gulf dividing northern (Athens) from southern (Sparta) Greece.

Calonice

              Yes, my dear,   95
we all would like to know what's so important.

Lysistrata

I'll tell you in a sec. But first I'll ask
you all a little question.

Calonice

              Go ahead.

Lysistrata

The fathers of your kids: they're off at war.
You miss them, right? I know that each of you   100
has got a husband fighting in the war.

Calonice

My husband's been away for five whole months.
The northern front. He's guarding his lieutenant.

Myrrhine

Mine's in the south, been gone for *seven* months.

Lampito

And mine, no sooner he come home from war,   105
he take his shield and mobilize again.

Lysistrata

And how about our lovers? They're gone too.
And since we don't get imports any more,
we can't even buy a decent twelve-inch dildo.
Well, it's not the real thing, but at least it's something.   110
So, are you ready, if I had a plan in mind,
to help me end the war?

Calonice

              By God, I'm ready!
I'd even pawn my best designer jeans
and use the proceeds only to celebrate!

Myrrhine

And you could cut me up just like a pizza,°   115
and everyone would get a slice of it!

Calonice

And I would climb the highest Spartan mountain:°
from there I'd see where they have hidden peace!

---

115 In Greek 'flatfish' (turbot), which resembles only half a fish. Plato apparently borrowed
      this joke for a memorable philosophical metaphor in Aristophanes' speech in *Symposium*.

117 Mount Taygetos, the highest mountain in the Spartan territory (Laconia).

Lysistrata

All right, I'll tell you. No need keeping secrets.
Well, women, if we're really serious   120
and want to make our husbands end the war,
we must swear off—

Calonice

Off what?

Lysistrata

You'll do it, then?

Calonice

We'll do it, even if it means our death!

Lysistrata

All right, here goes: we've got to swear off fucking.
Hey, where are you going? What's this backing off?   125
You shake your heads, you make a pickle-face.
How come you're all so pale? How come you're crying?
Are you with me or not? What do you want to do?

Calonice

I'm out. I guess I'll let the war drag on.

Myrrhine

Me too. I guess I'll let the war drag on.   130

Lysistrata

This from you, Ms. Pizza? You just said
you wanted us to slice you up in pieces.

Calonice

If there's anything else at all, that's fine. Through fire
I would even walk. But as for fucking, no.
There's nothing like it, dear Lysistrata.   135

Lysistrata

And you?

Wife

I guess I'll walk through fire too.

Lysistrata

Oh, what a low and shameless race are we!
No wonder men write tragedies about us.
We're nothing but a diaper and a bed.
But Lampito, comrade, surely you'll be willing.   140
If you alone would join me, we could do it!
What do you say?

Lampito
        Is definitely hard
for women to sleep alone without the penis.   )
But nevertheless we must. We need the peace.

Lysistrata
Oh, dearest comrade, manliest of women!   145

Calonice
Look, *if* we really swear off...what you say,
which God forbid, would that be really likely
to bring peace?

Lysistrata
        I am absolutely positive.
If we go home, and get ourselves made up,
and slip on one of our imported gowns   150
with nothing underneath, and show some crotch,
our husbands will get hard and want to screw;
but if we keep away and don't go near them,
they'll soon enough make peace, you have my word.

Lampito
Remember Helen of Troy, whose warrior husband°   155
looked at her naked tits and dropped his sword!

Calonice
But what if our husbands pay us no attention?

Lysistrata
As the saying goes, you've got to use your head.

Calonice
But that's no good, I wouldn't stoop to that.
And they might resort to violence, and drag us off   160
to the bedroom.

Lysistrata
        Then you'll have to grab the door-jamb.

Calonice
And if they beat us up?

---

155 Alluding to a memorable scene in Euripides' play *Andromache*, which followed the story
    of Helen and Menelaus on their return to Sparta after the Trojan War. The meeting of
    the betrayed husband and his faithless wife after the fall of Troy, when Menelaus did
    not have the nerve to kill her, was a favorite scene with painters. With typical daring,
    Euripides added Helen's breast-baring. This example of Spartan wimpishness must
    have cheered up the Athenians, and in terms of Lysistrata's scheme it is a well-chosen
    'historical' precedent.

Lysistrata

  Then don't cooperate.
Men don't enjoy it when they have to force you.
And make them suffer otherwise as well.
They'll give. There's never been a happy man   165
who doesn't have a peaceful married life.

Calonice

If you and Lampito want to, so do I.

Lampito

So: I am sure that we persuade our men
for peace with honor, nothing up the sleeve.°
But Athenians are a democratic mob:°   170
how you propose to get them to agree?

Lysistrata

Don't worry, I'll take care of the Athenians.

Lampito

But the military and industrial complex, °
your capital funds stored on the citadel!

Lysistrata

I tell you, I've anticipated that.   175
We're seizing the whole citadel today.
The old women took on that assignment.
They'll pretend to have religious business there.
They're at it now, while we conclude our plans.

Lampito

I must admit, your plan sounds quite complete.   180

---

169 Pro-war Athenians often claimed that Spartans did not negotiate truthfully or keep agreements.

170 Athenian democracy was a radically new form of government in the fifth century and was not universally applauded, even at Athens, where right-wing factions from some aristocratic families (the former ruling elite) hoped that it would be a short-lived experiment. Sparta lived under her traditional dual monarchy and perceived democracy as a dangerous threat to international order and stability. One of the great issues of the war was whether Athens should be allowed to spread democracy throughout Greece: the Athenian imperial policy was, wherever possible, to replace ruling elites with democratic governments. Anti-democractic states considered this 'mob-rule.'

173 The imperial democracy of Athens relied on its superior navy and its wealth during the war. In their disastrous defeat at Syracuse in 413 Athens had lost a lot of both, so that their enemies were now more than an equal match, but Aristophanes maintains the flattering self-image of his Athenian audience. The Athenian Treasuries were kept on the citadel (the Acropolis), under the protection of their city-goddess Athena: for her significance in the play see the Introduction.

Lysistrata
　Then, Lampito, let's swear an oath without
　delay, and then our plan will be official.

Lampito
　Propose the oath, and we all swear to it.

Lysistrata
　All right, then. Officeress! Where is she? Wake her up!°
　Put down your shield here. No, the other way.　　　　　185
　Now someone get a victim.

Calonice
　　　　　Say, Lysistrata,
　what sort of oath is this?

Lysistrata
　　　　　What sort of oath?
　A slaughter in a shield, like tragic ones,
　the fatted calf: you know.

Calonice
　　　　　We can't do that,
　we shouldn't use a shield if we want peace.　　　　　190

Lysistrata
　What's *your* suggestion, smarty?

Calonice
　　　　　I suggest,
　we get a full-grown cock and slaughter that.

Lysistrata
　You've got a one-track mind.

Calonice
　　　　　But then what *will*
　we swear on?

Lysistrata
　　　　　Something's hit me. Want to hear?
　Let's chuck the shield and get a giant wine-glass,　　　195
　and slaughter a great big bottle of red bordeaux,
　and swear we'll never fill the glass with water!

Lampito
　Oh da! One cannot quarrel with that oath.

184　The Athenians used slave-archers, mostly from Western Asia, as police and as security
　　guards for officials like the Magistrate who appears later (387 ff.). Lysistrata has a female
　　version.

Lysistrata
  So someone get the bottle and the glass.

Myrrhine
  Oh God, girls, take a look at all that glassware!   200

Calonice
  And just to touch this bottle makes me come!

Lysistrata
  So put it down! Join hands, now, everyone.
  O Goddess of Persuasion, Conspiratorial Glass:
  receive this offering from the wives. Amen.

Calonice
  Behold the color of the gurgling blood.   205

Lampito
  Perceive the sweetness of its fair aroma.

Myrrhine
  I'd like to be the first to take the oath.

Calonice
  Hey, not so fast, you've got to wait your turn.

Lysistrata
  No! *All* hands on the glass. You also, Lampito.   210
  Let one of you repeat the oath I make,
  and everybody else swear her allegiance.
  I won't allow my lover or my husband—

Calonice
  I won't allow my lover or my husband—

Lysistrata
  to get near me with a hard-on. I can't hear you!

Calonice
  to get near me with a hard-on. Oh my God!   215
  My knees are getting weak, Lysistrata!

Lysistrata
  At home my life will be completely chaste.

Calonice
  At home my life will be completely chaste.

Lysistrata
  I'll wear my sexiest dresses and cosmetics—

Calonice
  I'll wear my sexiest dresses and cosmetics—   220

Lysistrata
  to make my man as horny as can be.

Calonice
to make my man as horny as can be.

Lysistrata
But never will I willingly give in.

Calonice
But never will I willingly give in.

Lysistrata
If he should get his way by violence—   225

Calonice
If he should get his way by violence—

Lysistrata
I'll simply lie there uncooperative.

Calonice
I'll simply lie there uncooperative.

Lysistrata
I will not wrap my legs around his back—

Calonice
I will not wrap my legs around his back—   230

Lysistrata
nor will I crouch down like a lioness.

Calonice
nor will I crouch down like a lioness.

Lysistrata
As I drink this wine, so will I keep this oath—

Calonice
As I drink this wine, so will I keep this oath—

Lysistrata
but if I break it, may the wine be water.   235

Calonice
but if I break it, may the wine be water.

Lysistrata
So say you one and all?

All
So say we all!

Lysistrata
All right, I'll do the honors.

Calonice
Just make sure
you take one share: we must have solidarity.

Lampito
  What's that?

Lysistrata
  The signal: as I said before,   240
  the ladies who would seize the citadel.
  They've done it already! Listen, Lampito:
  return to Sparta now, and start the strike.
  And leave these women here as hostages.
  The rest of us will enter the citadel   245
  and lock the gates and barricade ourselves.

Calonice
  But don't you think the men will try to stop us?
  And pretty quickly?

Lysistrata
          They don't worry me.
  They'll come with torches, shouting and making threats,
  but they can't make us open up these gates   250
  until they promise to honor our demands.

Calonice
  By Sex and Love they can't!° For otherwise,
  we're nothing but a weak and gutless gender.

Men's Chorus

Leader
  Come on, sergeant, get a move on,
    even if your shoulder's raw
  Hefting all this heavy wood and
    dragging all of it uphill.   255

Chorus (1¹)°
  Incredible and shocking too
    for wives to act like this!
  We fed and clothed them: now we find
    they're dirty terrorists!   260

  They seized the City Treasury
    and Offices of State.
  They occupy our holy ground
    and won't unlock the gate!   265

---

252 She swears by Aphrodite, the goddess of sexual enjoyment.
256 Greek dramatic choruses (the songs and dances performed in the orchestra by the chorus)
     were normally strophic, that is, composed in two or more strophes (stanzas) that had
     the same rhythmical structure. In this translation, each chorus is numbered (there are
     eight) and each strophe comprising a chorus is numbered by superscript: this is the first
     strophe of the first chorus.

Leader

    Butts in gear, men, double-time it,
      stack them right against the gate;
    then we'll pile them all around it,
      sealing in the enemy troops:
    every single female traitor
      party to this coup d' etat.
    Then we'll make a giant bonfire:
      toss your flares at my command.
    Death by burning is our verdict,
      starting with the bitch in charge.°   270

Chorus (1²)

    While we're alive they'll never have
      the laugh on this old geezer!
    Remember when the Spartans first °
      attempted such a seizure?   275

    They came on big but went out small,
      their reputation shot.
    We didn't even let them keep
      a rag to wipe their snot!   280

Leader

    Ranks in order, siege positions,
      just the way we did it then.
    Let these women beat us now and
      all our reputation's gone.°   285

---

270 They mention the wife of the wealthy Lykon. She was apparently known for her scandalous living: the comic poets frequently joke about her extravagance and adulteries. Her name was probably Rhodia, but this also means 'woman from Rhodes' (implying non-Athenian ancestry) and so might have been a nickname whose significance is now lost.

274 In 508 a Spartan force under King Cleomenes I came to Athens and seized the Acropolis in support of Isagoras in his power-struggle with Cleisthenes, a founding hero of the democracy, who accepted the Spartans' surrender after a two-day siege. During the play the old men boast of having taken part in battles that would make them well over 100 years old: too old for realism but not too old for their characterization as men who had struggled to establish the democracy, which was popularly thought to have begun with the fall of the last Athenian tyrant in 510 (1150 n.).

285 They allude to the battle of Marathon in 490, when a Persian expeditionary force under Darius and guided by the ousted Athenian tyrant Hippias (1150 n.) landed at the Bay of Marathon and marched toward Athens, 26 miles SW. At the town of Marathon they were met and defeated by an Athenian-Plataiean army. This victory, considered by Athenians to be their most glorious, ended Darius' European ambitions, and the Persians did not invade again for ten years, when they returned under Xerxes. Later legend told how one Phidippides (or Philippides) ran back to Athens to announce the good news. Although he reportedly dropped dead of fatigue as soon as he had done so, the marathon race still commemorates his run.

Chorus (2¹)

The goal of our journey's around the bend.
but the steepest part's at the very end.
Our shoulders are aching, we're out of fuel.
It would have been smarter to bring a mule.   290

But keep it moving all the same,
and don't forget to fan the flame.
There's little point in climbing higher,
then finding out we've lost our fire.
God, the smoke!   295

Chorus (2²)

The smoke's rushing out like a raving bitch
and biting our eyes with an awful itch.
Can't see where we're going: it seems to us
we're climbing the slopes of Vesuvius.   300

But hurry onward anyhow:
We've got to save the goddess now!
Our Purple Hearts aren't worth a dime
unless we help her out this time.
God, the smoke!   305

Leader

Now the fire's burning lively,
  now the gods are on our side.
Stack the logs and set your torches,
  then we'll charge the gate like rams,   310
Open up, you wives, or else we'll
  burn the gates and smoke you out.
Place the logs in orderly fashion.
  Ah, this smoke is terrible!
Can't the generals hear us? Won't they
  lift some logs? Our arms are dead.
Pot of Coals, it's up to you now: 315
  furnish fire; I'll lead the charge.
Victory Goddess,° lend assistance,
  help us beat these mutinous wives!

---

317 The Victory Goddess (Nike) had a shrine on the Acropolis that was part of the massive
building program undertaken by the democracy under Pericles and whose construction
had been competed some ten years earlier. The shrine still stands today. The cult of Nike,
decreed in the 440's, was democratically organized (its priestess being elected or allotted
from among all citizen women). By contrast, Lysistrata and her women align themselves
with the citadel-goddess Athena Polias, whose cult was older than the democracy and
was run by women from high-born families.

Women's Chorus

Women's Leader
I think I see the smoke and rising flames!
The siege is underway. We've got to hurry! 320

Chorus (3¹)
Faster, faster, we've got to fly,
  or else our friends will surely die!
Some nasty elders have got a view
  to hold a female barbecue! 325

We started early but might be late:
  we had to fill our pitchers.
The well was jammed, we got delayed
  by slaves and pushy bitches, 330

shouting, shoving, smashing pots,
  banging heads and raising knots.
Now we're here with pitchers filled
  to keep our friends from being grilled. 335

Chorus (3²)
There they are, the demented bums!
  They're stacking logs to burn our chums,
shouting threats of an awful kind,
  to leave but ash and smoke behind. 340

O Goddess,° spare the women's life!
  They occupied your temple
to save the Greeks from war and strife
  and madness pure and simple. 345

Be our ally, help defend
  women fighting evil men.
Help us with our pitchers filled
  to keep our friends from getting grilled.

Women's Leader
Hold it, girls! What's this I see here? 350
  Men, and evil bastards too.

Men's Leader
What the hell is going on here?
  Where's this swarm of women from?

Women
Scared of us? We're not so many.
  Still, there's more where we came from. 355

---

341 They pray to Athena Polias (317 n.).

Men
>Boys, do you hear all this babble?
>>Someone bash her with a log.

Women
>Put your pitchers on the ground, girls:
>>looks as if they want a fight.

Men
>How'd you like to have your mouth shut?   360
>>Two or three punches ought to do.

Women
>Come on, hit me: I'm not moving.
>>I would love to chew your balls.

Men
>Quiet, or I'll bust your wrinkles!

Women
>Go ahead, just lift your hand.   365

Men
>What about my knuckles? What then?

Women
>Want to have your guts pulled out?

Men
>Tragic poets have a saying:
>>nothing's wilder than a woman!

Women
>Come on, girls, let's lift our pitchers.   370

Men
>What's this water for, you bitch?

Women
>What's this fire, you mausoleum?

Men
>Just a pyre for your friends.

Women
>I'm about to douse your pyre.

Men
>Douse it?

Women
>That's exactly right.   375

Men
>How'd you like your hair on fire?

Women

　　Get some soap: I've got your bath.

Men

　　Bath, you crone?

Women

　　　　You really need one.

Men

　　Listen to her!

Women

　　　　I've a right.

Men

　　Quiet!

Women

　　You're not judge and jury now.°　　　　　　　　　　　380

Men

　　Burn her hair!

Women

　　　　And now the bath!

Men

　　Goddamn!

Women

　　　　I hope we didn't scald you.

Men

　　Scald us? Stop! We've had enough!

Women

　　Maybe now you'll start to blossom.

380　'You're not judge and jury now.' In democratic Athens, full popular sovereignty was rooted in the court system, where individuals brought lawsuits or prosecutions personally (there were no official prosecutors or advocates). Cases were heard by large juries that represented the whole people and whose verdict was final. At the age of thirty any males citizen could be a juror, but at this time most jurors were poor and/or old men. One reason was that the young men were away at war. Another was that under Pericles the democracy had begun to pay jurors for service. This made jury-service attractive to men unfit for more remunerative occupations, so that it became in effect a welfare payment for the urban poor and a pension for the old. This arrangement created friction between the generations and social classes (many litigants were wealthy and powerful men who resented being at the mercy of a 'mob'), and it was open to political abuses: all these are explored by Aristophanes in his play *Wasps*. Later in our play the men complain that the women's seizure of the citadel has cut off their pay (625), and the women reply by calling them freeloaders (646 ff.). Since the jurors were essentially the same people who supported the war-policy, Aristophanes attempts to arouse the audience's resentment by calling attention to their low social status and their selfish interests.

Men

No, we'll wither up instead.   385

Women

You brought the fire: warm yourselves.

SCENE II

Magistrate°

I hear our spoiled wives are out of hand.
Another phony festival for their wine-god,°
a noisy rooftop party for Adonis,°
just like the one that spoiled our assembly.   390
That ill-starred, foolish politician moved
we sail to Sicily,° while his wife was dancing
and yelling for Adonis. When he said,
let's muster allied troops for this armada,
his wife was on the rooftop getting drunk   395
and yelling 'Oh doomed youth!' But he persisted,
the goddamned stubborn hotheaded son of a bitch!
That's just the kind of mischief wives can make!

Men's Leader

And wait till I tell you what they did to *us*.
They treated us like slaves and dumped their pitchers   400
all over us and soaked our clothes through,
so anyone would say we pissed our pants!

Magistrate

It serves your right, I swear by the salty sea-god.
We men have only got ourselves to blame.
We virtually teach our wives to misbehave,   405
and so they're always nurturing their plots.
What do we say when we visit the marketplace?
'Oh, goldsmith, about that locket I bought from you.
My wife was having a ball the other night
and it seems this bolt here slipped right out of its hole.   410

---

387   Magistrate: see Introduction.
388   This wine (or beer) god, Sabazius, was a foreign import not recognized by the city and
      popular with 'outsiders', like women, slaves and the poor.
389   Adonis was another foreign import not recognized by the city. His cult was celebrated
      by women in spring or summer on rooftops: the women planted quickly flowering and
      quickly withering gardens and lamented the death of the youth Adonis, favorite of
      Aphrodite.
392   For the doomed Sicilian Expedition, see Introduction. Since the assembly was deciding
      to send the flower of Athenian youth into a great battle, the lamentations for Adonis
      were remembered after the disaster as a bad omen.

I've got to leave, I'm travelling up to Bangor.°
I'd be grateful if you'd visit her some night
with the proper tool and fix the hole that needs it.'
Another husband visits his local shoemaker,
a half-grown boy with a very full-grown cock.   415
'Say, shoemaker, about this pair of slippers:
my wife complains the orifice grips too tight;
her skin is very soft. While I'm at work,
please loosen up her orifice a bit.'
It's this complacency that leads to trouble,   420
so here I am, a supplier for the army,
in need of public funds,° and now I find
the women have shut me out of the treasury!
I'm wasting time. You slaves, bring on the crowbars!
I'll put a stop to all this female foolery.   425
You bozo, look alive! And you as well!
Stop wondering if they're any bars around.°
Pick up those crowbars, take them to the gate,
and pry it open. Here, I'll show you how,
I'll help you pry.

Lysistrata
        No need for any prying.   430
I'm coming out myself. No need for crowbars.
We don't need force, but rather brains and sense.

Magistrate
That so, you bitch? I'm calling a policeman.°
Arrest this woman, put the handcuffs on.

Lysistrata
By the goddess, if he lays a hand on me,   435
policeman or no policeman, he'll regret it.

Magistrate
Can you be scared of her? Go on and grab her.
And you there, help him out. Hogtie the woman!

Old Woman A
By the goddess, if you even raise your hand
to her, I'll beat you till you shit your pants!   440

---

411 'To Salamis,' an Attic island which for Athenians had sexual associations, apparently
     because the Salaminians' oarsmanship on small boats reminded them of women on top
     in sexual intercourse.
423 Aristophanes implies that public officials steal the city's money, a charge made explicit
     at 490-1.
427 Comic slaves are conventionally fond of drinking.
433 For the policemen see 184 n.

Magistrate
> What, shit my pants? Another policeman here!
> Grab this one first, the one with the dirty mouth.

Old Woman B
> By the goddess, if you lay a fingertip
> on her, you'll need an icebag for both eyes.

Magistrate
> Where'd *she* come from? Police! Arrest this woman!   445
> Whoever's on this outing I'll arrest.

Old Woman C
> By the goddess, if you make a move toward her,
> I'll pull your hair out until you're bloody bald.

Magistrate
> My god, I'm out of cops! I'm in a fix.
> I *cannot* let myself be screwed by women!   450
> We need a full-scale charge. Attention, Huns!°
> Prepare to charge!

Lysistrata
>   As you will quickly see,
> we too have troops, four companies of women:
> they're fully armed and on alert inside.

Magistrate
> Go forward, Huns, and twist their arms behind them!   455

Lysistrata
> Come forward, allied women, on the double!
> You market-women,° meter-maids, bag-ladies!
> You check-out girls, mud-wrestlers, waitresses!
> Attack them, stomp them, chew them, beat them up!
> Cease fire! Stand at ease, don't chase them down!   460

Magistrate
> Alas, my Huns are utterly defeated.

Lysistrata
> But what did you expect? Did you imagine
> that we were slaves, or did you think that women
> can't show courage?

---

451 These archer-police are from Scythia (the modern Ukraine).

456 'Market-women,' who were conventionally older women, had stalls in the marketplace
and were poor citizens, resident aliens or slaves. Those singled out here are sellers of
wild herbs, porridge, garlic, bread, rooms at inns (which included prostitutes): the social
equivalents of the types listed in the translation. They were stereotyped in comedy as
bold, loud and abusive, so that they make perfect 'soldiers' for Lysistrata .

Magistrate

>   Courage, yes indeed,   465
> provided there's a lot of booze inside 'em.

Men's Leader

> Why waste your breath, my Magistrate,
>   why argue with these bitches?
> You know the kind of bath we took
>   without that kind of soft soap.   470

Women's Leader

> Dear sir, it's impolite to raise
>   your hand against your neighbors.
> Try that again, we'll punch you out,
>   though we prefer decorum.
> We promise to be meek as girls,
>   so don't stir up a mare's nest.   475

Men's Chorus (4¹)

> King of the gods, these women are beasts!
> We need a plan, to say the least!
> Let's try to find out
> what they're angry about,
> why they're raising hell   480
> on our sacred citadel.

Men's Leader

> Now question her and test her answers,
>   and don't be buffaloed.
> It's bad enough they've gone this far;
>   we mustn't let it go!   485

Magistrate

> First I'd like to know the reason
>   why you took the citadel.

Lysistrata

> Confiscation of the money:
>   thus we put a stop to war.

Magistrate

> Money's causing war?

Lysistrata

>   Exactly:
> also the political mess.
> Generals and politicians°   490

---

490 She singles out Pisander, the only named politician abused in the play. For his topical
     importance see Introduction.

argue war so they can steal.
Go ahead and fight, but henceforth
no more money leaves this place.

Magistrate
You will keep it.

Lysistrata
No, we'll save it.

Magistrate
Save it?

Lysistrata
What's so strange in that?
Don't we manage household money?°   495

Magistrate
Not the same.

Lysistrata
How so?

Magistrate
It's war!

Lysistrata
Stop the war.

Magistrate
Then who will save us?

Lysistrata
We will.

Magistrate
You?

Lysistrata
That's right.

Magistrate
My god!

Lysistrata
What's your choice?

Magistrate
You're mad!

Lysistrata
Be angry.
Nonetheless we must.

---

495 For wives as domestic managers see Introduction.

Magistrate
No way!   500

Lysistrata
Must.

Magistrate
If I refuse?

Lysistrata
I'd like that!

Magistrate
Dare you speak of war and peace?

Lysistrata
Yes.

Magistrate
So make it fast.

Lysistrata
I'll do that.
Calm yourself.

Magistrate
It's difficult:
itchy fists.

Old Woman A.
You risk a beating.   505

Magistrate
Shut up, bag. *You* talk.

Lysistrata
I will.°
All along we kept our silence,
acquiesced as nice wives should—
or else!—although we didn't like it.
You would escalate the war;
we would ask you so politely,
even though it hurt inside,   510
'Darling, what's the latest war-news?
What did all you men decree?
Anything about a treaty?'
Then you'd say, 'What's that to you?
Shut up!' And I'd shut up.

---

507 Lysistrata's account of dispute between wives and husbands over the war is inspired by
the famous conversation between Hector and Andromache in the sixth book of Homer's
Iliad.

Old Woman B

          Not me!   515

Magistrate

  Then I'd smack you!

Lysistrata

             There you are.
Then we'd hear some even worse news,
  so we'd say, 'How stupid, dear!'
Then you'd give us dirty looks and
  say, 'Go mend my cloak or else!°   520
War is strictly for the menfolk.'

Magistrate

  Right we were.

Lysistrata

            You stupid fool!
We were quite prepared to warn you;
  you refused to hear advice.
Then disaster. Throughout the city
  'All our boys are gone!' you cried.
That's when all the wives decided
  we must act to save the Greeks.   525
Thus we're here: no point in waiting.
  Want to hear some good advice?
Shut your mouth the way *we* used to,
  let us save you from yourselves.

Magistrate

You save *us*? That's madness!

Lysistrata

                    Shut up!

Magistrate

  Me shut up for you? You skirt!   530
  Let me die before that happens!

Lysistrata

  It's my skirt that bothers you?
  Give the man a skirt and bonnet:
  Maybe that will shut him up.

ᵉʳ gender roles were conventionally expressed by the antithesis weaving/fighting.
ʲtrata will presently reverse these roles by dressing the Magistrate like a wife and
ing him to weave. The women claim that their domestic work is a better model for
ng the city than male fighting skills.

Old Woman C
　　Here's a sewing basket also!　　　　　　　　　　535

Lysistrata
　　Now he needs some chewing gum.
　　Put a little lipstick on him,
　　　stuff your hankies down his shirt.
　　War is strictly for the women!

Women's Leader
　　Women arise, let go your jars.
　　It's time to help these friends of ours.　　　　　540

Women's Chorus (4²)
　　I'm dancing forever, I'll never retreat,
　　never be tired or get cold feet!
　　I'm ready to strive
　　for the cause of the wives,
　　who are decent, smart,　　　　　　　　　　　　545
　　patriotic, bold of heart!

Women's Leader
　　Most valiant child of bold fore-mothers,
　　　no slow-down or retreat!
　　You've got him where you want him now:
　　　you're in the driver's seat!　　　　　　　　　550

Lysistrata
　　Goddess of sex and sweet desire,°
　　　breathe upon our breasts and flanks,
　　give our husbands lasting hard-ons,
　　　help us make them leave the ranks.

Magistrate
　　What's your plan?

Lysistrata
　　　　　My first requirement:　　　　　　　　　555
　　soldiers leave the marketplace.

Old Woman A
　　Hear, hear!

Lysistrata
　　　　　They strut about in armor,
　　pushing shoppers, smashing goods.

Magistrate
　　Manly men!

551　For Aphrodite see 252 n.

Lysistrata
>But pretty comic,
>stacking burgers on their shields.   560

Old Woman B
>God, I've seen those grand lieutenants
>use their helmets for a bowl.
>Mercenaries slap the salesgirls,
>>never even pay their bill!

Magistrate
>*You* can stop these wartime hardships,   565
>>I'm to gather?

Lysistrata
>>>Sure!

Magistrate
>>>>And how?

Lysistrata
>Open up your sewing basket:
>>see the skein of tangled wool?
>Put it to the spindle this way,
>>wind it here, now wind it there.   570
>Thus the war can be unravelled,
>>making truces here, and there.

Magistrate
>Skiens and spindles? I don't get it.

Lysistrata
>Sense and skill is all you need.

Magistrate
>Show me.

Lysistrata
>Gladly. First you wash the
>city as we wash the wool,
>cleaning out the bullshit.° Then we   575
>>pluck away the parasites;
>break up strands that clump together,
>>forming special interest groups;
>Here's a bozo: squeeze his head off.
>Now you're set to card the wool:

---

575 Comic poets like to portray social and political problems as being the fault of a small
number of selfish and disruptive people—including current political leaders—and suggest that, if these people could be eliminated, all would be well and ordinary people
(like most spectators) could live their lives in peace.

use your basket for the carding,
  the basket of solidarity.
There we put our migrant workers,   580
  foreign friends, minorities,
immigrants and wage-slaves, every
  person useful to the state.
Don't forget our allies, either,
  languishing like separate strands.
Bring it all together now, and
  make one giant ball of yarn.   585
Now you're ready: weave a brand new
  suit for all the citizens.

Magistrate
  War is not the same as wool-balls!
    What do women know of war?

Lysistrata
  Even more than you do, asshole.
    First of all we make the children,
  Then we send them off to war, then—

Magistrate
  That's enough! I take your point.   590

Lysistrata
  What about young wives? They waste their
    prime of life in solitude.
  What about the girls who'll grow old
    long before they find a man?

Magistrate
  Men get old too.

Lysistrata
            That's quite different.
  Men can always get a girl,
even greybeards. Girls don't have that   595
  luxury. Their time is short.
Men won't marry older girls: they
  pine away in spinsterhood.

Magistrate
  Lucky men! For us it's easy:
    all we need is in our pants!

Lysistrata
  Time for you to die, old geezer.
  Fetch your coffin. Here's a grave-site.   600

We'll arrange the funeral.
Put a lily in his hand.

Old Woman C

Here's a wreath.

Old Woman A

And here's a bible.

Lysistrata

What are you waiting for? You're dead!   605
Off to the big bureaucracy in the sky.
You're holding up St. Peter.°

Magistrate

You haven't heard the last of this. Outrageous!
By god, I'll show the other magistrates
exactly what you've done to me. So there!   610

Lysistrata

I hope you won't complain about your funeral.
We did our best. I tell you what: we'll hold
a proper service at your grave: a dance!

Men's Chorus

Men's Leader

Wake up men, defend our manhood!
    Strip for action! Dance away!   615

Chorus (5¹)

There's more to this outbreak
    than you might guess:
we're sure that these women
    are terrorists!°

The Spartans have managed
    to infiltrate   620
our houses and women:
    and next the state!

The citadel-seizure
    we understand:

---

607 'St. Peter': Charon, who ferried the souls of the dead across the underworld River Styx
     to Hades where the dead were popularly thought to dwell as shades.
619 They accuse the women of the actionable offense of plotting tyranny (1150 n.), that is,
     of conspiring to change the democratic constitution in order to limit power to certain
     individuals or groups. Popular politicians frequently implied that their opponents
     (especially upper-class ones) were potential 'tyrants' in order to distract attention from
     substantive issues, just as their modern counterparts imply that an opponent is unpatri-
     otic. Aristophanes regularly pokes fun at these techniques in trying to alert the audience
     to their shallowness and political divisiveness.

They're putting an end to
  our pension plan!°   625

Leader

Outrageous that these women dare to prate
of war and peace and governing the state!
And then they tell us we should make a deal
with Spartans, who are slipperier than an eel!
It's nothing but a plan for tyranny.   630
While I'm alive they won't do that to me.
I'll fight these women with my dying breath.
For I say, Give me liberty or give me death!°
I'm standing tall, a loyal patriot:
if you don't like it I'll kick you in the butt!   635

Women's Chorus

Women's Leader

You'll soon be running home to mommy.
Strip for action, girls, and dance!

Chorus (5²)

A debt to our country
  we must repay:
so we've good advice for
  you all today.

we're healthy and happy
  and well-to-do,
and all our successes
  we owe to you.   640

Our schools and our temples,°
  our social lives:

---

625 See 380 n.

633 They quote from a patriotic drinking-song recalling Harmodius and his friend Aristogiton, who assassinated Hipparchus, the brother of the tyrant Hippias (1150 n.) in 514. These two were popularly revered as founding fathers of democracy, but among the educated upper-classes it was said that they were in reality not freedom-fighters but a pair of lovers avenging a personal insult (Thucydides 6.53 ff.).

641 The women claim the right to offer advice because they have managed their households better than the men have managed the city and because they bore the sons who have been sent to war. Here they list city cults connected with the preparation of young girls for domestic management and for child-rearing. These were the old and elite cults of Athena Polias (317 n.) and Artemis of Brauron, which predated the democracy and were run by aristocratic families. The girls who took part, though they represented all Athenian girls, were chosen only from such families. Aristophanes maintains the contrast between the high-born, educated women and the poor, ignorant men.

they all helped to make us
  your perfect wives.   645

Leader

With good advice we want to pay you back.°
Don't worry that it comes from Jill not Jack.
Consider it on its merits. Anyway,   650
we bear the children and deserve our say.
What contribution do these old men make?
They never seem to give, but only take.
We pay for all their laws, their wars, their theft.
And they'll keep taking till there's nothing left.   655
Old men, I warn you: better hold your peace.
You make a sound, we'll kick you in the teeth!

Men's Chorus (6¹)

I've seen a lot of arrogance,
  but this outdoes it all.
We've got to beat them down to size
  if we've still got the balls.   660

Leader

Take your shirts off, you're not tacos!
  Let them whiff your manly smell!   665

Chorus

We once were Athenian raiders,°
we dealt mercilessly with traitors.
  Let's do it again,
  pretend we're young men,   670
not washed-up old alligators!

Leader

We can't afford to let them get the jump,°
for women are a match for any hump.
They might build submarines and strike below:
we wouldn't know just when to expect the blow.   675
We'd hate to face equestrian encounters,
for women are indomitable mounters.
You'll never shake them off once they get on:

646 For the old men as freeloaders, see 380 n.
666 They continue their recollection of the struggle against tyranny (1150 n.), alluding to the battle of Leipsydrion, where in the period after the murder of Hipparchus (633 n.) the tyrant Hippias besieged his opponents. After a hard fight Hippias defeated them, but their exploit was later celebrated in a patriotic song. The old men here seem to have got their history wrong, speaking as if they had been the victors, as in the action against Cleomenes (274 n.).
672 Sailing and horsemanship were very commonly used for sexual metaphors and jokes.

just look at pictures of the Amazons!°
We must move now to make their plot a wreck,   680
so let's move out and grab them by the neck!

Women's Chorus (6²)

Go on and get our fire going,
  and pull the bitch's tail!
Then all your buddies get to hear
  how loud you weep and wail.   685

Leader

Take your skirts off, don't be modest!
  Let them whiff an angry sow!   690

Chorus

We wait for the note of your clarion,
you nattering octogenarian!
  Just give us a chance
  to pull down your pants
and deliver your balls by caesarean.°   695

Leader

And anyway your efforts are for naught:
the wives are carrying out a foolproof plot.
Pass all the laws you want and call for war:
the decent folks will only hate you more.   700
Just yesterday I had a picnic planned
for a lovely visitor from a foreign land,
in fact a pot of Theban caviar!°
But nothing doing: that's against your law.
You'll keep on regulating us, no doubt,
till someone picks you up and throws you out.   705

SCENE III

Hail, leader of our common enterprise!
But why emerge? How come you look so sad?

Lysistrata

The wives reveal their baseness and grow weak.
It's got me down, I don't know what to do.

---

679 The Amazons were mythical women who fought like men and long ago, in the time of the legendary Athenian King Theseus, had invaded Athens and occupied the citadel. This incident was the subject of a well-known public mural by the painter Micon.
695 The old women allude to midwifery, a usual occupation of their age-group, and to a fable in which the lowly beetle avenges the loss of its young by breaking the eagle's eggs (here metaphorical for testicles).
702 They had invited 'a lovely well-bred girl—an eel from Thebes' (36 n.).

Leader
What's that you say? 710

Lysistrata
It's true, it's true.

Leader
Let's hear it all: we're friends that you can trust.

Lysistrata
A shame to speak but risky to keep quiet.

Leader
Don't hide a crisis that affects us all!

Lysistrata
I'll make it short: they're dying to get laid. 715

Leader
Oh gods!

Lysistrata
I doubt the gods can get us out of this.
I certainly can't keep on withholding wives
from husbands: they're determined to escape.
I caught one by that grotto with a shovel,
scraping away and widening her hole. 720
Another one was climbing on that pulley,
pulling herself off. And another one
got on a giant bird, said 'take me to
a whorehouse!'° Luckily I grabbed her hair. 725
And every excuse for going home there is,
they make. I think that's one of them right now.
Hey you, where to?

Wife A
       I've got to run back home.
My bolts of woolen cloth, the finest kind,
are very much in need of moth-balls.

Lysistrata
         Moth-balls? 730
Get back in there!

Wife
      I swear I'll come right back.
Just let me spread my wool out on the bed.

---

725 'To Orsilochus' house': he was apparently a pimp, and the name (which suggests erection) may be his trade-name: another pimp, whose real name was Philostratus, is referred to in 957 as 'Dogfox'.

Lysistrata
You won't be spreading anything, nor be leaving.

Wife
But then my wool will go to waste!

Lysistrata
                                        So be it.

Wife B
Oh stupid me, forgetting to tenderize   735
the meat. I've got to go and beat it.

Lysistrata
                              Here's
another who forgot to beat her meat.
Get back inside!

Wife
                    I swear I'll be right back.
Just let me roll it in my hands a bit.

Lysistrata
No! Keep your hands to yourself. If you do this,   740
then all the wives will want to do the same.

Wife C
O Goddess of Labor, hold my pains a while,
till I can get to a proper birthing place!°

Lysistrata
What's all this yelling?

Wife
                        I'm having a baby now!

Lysistrata
But yesterday you were skinny.

Wife
                                Not today.   745
I've got to see the doctor, dear Lysistrata:
please send me home.

Lysistrata
                        Let's have a look at you.
What's this? It sounds like metal.

Wife
                              It's a boy!

---

743   Childbirth in sanctuaries (like the Acropolis) was ritually forbidden.

Lysistrata
I'd swear you've got some hollow metal thing
beneath your dress. Let's pull it up and see.   750
You card! You've got Athena's helmet there!°
Are you still pregnant?

Wife
                    Yes indeed I am.

Lysistrata
Then what's the helmet for?

Wife
                    In case the baby
comes while I'm still here. Then I'd deliver it
into the helmet, like a nesting bird.   755

Lysistrata
Preposterous, an obvious excuse.
You'll have to exercise the nesting option.

Wife C
I can't get any sleep here on the citadel,
not since I saw the Goddess' sacred snake!

Wife D
I can't sleep either. I toss and turn all night,   760
what with the hooting of the sacred owls.

Lysistrata
Enough! I won't hear any more excuses!
You miss your husbands, fine. But don't you know
they miss you too? I'm sure the nights they spend
are miserably lonely. Please hold out,   765
please bear with me a little while longer.
I've got a prophecy here predicting victory,°
provided we stay together. Want to hear it?

Wife A
Let's hear the prophecy.

---

751 The helmet on the great chryselephantine statue of Athena Promachos in the Parthenon, another part of the Periclean building program (317 n.) and therefore associated with the democracy and its war-policy.

767 Oracles and prophecies, written in archaic language and verse, were very popular (especially during the war) and were often used by politicians to enhance their platforms, much as polls and other statistical 'predictors' are today. Educated people like Aristophanes scoffed at prophecies and considered those who used them to be demagogues and those who trusted them to be gullible. Thus Lysistrata is not consistently above using demagogic tactics. The dumb wives are an appropriate audience: Aristophanes implies that any spectators who believe such appeals are as gullible as these wives.

Lysistrata
> Be quiet then.
> Yea, when the birds shall hole up in a single place,   770
> fleeing the eagles and keeping themselves quite chaste,
> then shall their problems be solved, they'll be on top,
> so says the King of the Gods—

Wife B
> We'll be on top?

Lysistrata
> But: if the birds start to argue and fly away
> down from the citadel holy, all will say: 775
> no bird more disgusting and shameless lives today!

Wife
> A pretty explicit prophecy. My god!

Lysistrata
> So let's hear no more talk of backing out.
> We'll all go back inside, for what a shame,
> dear friends, if we betray the prophecy.   780

Men's Chorus (7¹)

> I want to tell you all a tale.
>   I heard it as a lad.
> Once there was a man called Black,°
>   who lived as a nomad.   785
> A faithful dog his company,
>   he hunted and he roamed,
> he made his nets and set his traps
>   but never would go home.   790
>
> Because he hated women so,
>   and that's where he was wise.
> We follow Black's example in
>   that women we despise!   795

Men's Leader
> How about a kiss, old ghoul?

Women's Leader
> Wash your mouth out first, you fool!

Men's Leader
> I've got something for you here.

---

784 Melanion was a mythological figure who resembled Hippolytus (the hero of Euripides' play), being a lone hunter devoted to a virgin goddess (Atalanta who in another tradition was his bride).

Women's Leader
　　All I see is pubic hair.　　　　　　　　　　　　800

Men's Leader
　　That's right, I'm bushy down below.
　　But manly men are always so!°
　　Whenever I display my buns,
　　the enemy drops his spear and runs!

Women's Chorus (7²)
　　Our hero answers all your tales　　　　　　　805
　　　　about that other dope.
　　His name was Timon° and he was
　　　　a total misanthrope.

　　He wandered in the mountains too,
　　　　and acted very mean.　　　　　　　　810
　　If anybody crossed his path
　　　　he'd pick their carcass clean.

　　He couldn't stand men's evil ways,　　　　815
　　　　but women he enjoyed.°
　　We too stand up for principles,
　　　　of which you are devoid.　　　　　　　820

Women's Leader
　　You want me to re-do your nose?

Men's Leader
　　No way, it doesn't need your blows.

Women's Leader
　　So what about a stomping, then?

Men's Leader
　　Your bush resembles a pig-pen.

Women's Leader
　　You liar! That's a blatant slander!　　　　825
　　Just go ahead and take a gander:

801　He mentions two dead generals, Myronides and Phormion, who were heroes of the
　　　democracy and were remembered as tough commanders.

807　Timon of Athens, probably legendary, was the archetypal misanthrope (a man who be-
　　　comes fed up with society and deserts it) and inspired a long-lived literary and dramatic
　　　type. In recent years the fantasy of simply 'dropping out' (encouraged by the long war)
　　　had inspired several plays on this theme, including Aristophanes' *Birds*. A new example
　　　that has come to light in recent times is the fourth-century play *Dyskolos* ('The Grouch')
　　　by Menander.

816　The women embroider their version of Timon's story, for he is elsewhere portrayed as
　　　hating women as well as men.

my hair may be as white as snow,
but I keep myself well-groomed below.

SCENE IV

Lysistrata
Hey, women, women, come and take a look!
Come quick!

Wife
      What's happening? What's the fuss about?   830

Lysistrata
A man is coming. By the look of him
he's suffering from satyriasis.
O Goddess of Love and Pangs of Sweet Desire,
make this man's journey straight and very upright!

Wife
Where is he, whoever it is?

Lysistrata
               He's by that cave.   835

Wife
I see him now! Who is he?

Lysistrata
          Anyone know?

Myrrhine
Oh god, I do! That's my own husband, Rod!°

Lysistrata
You've got to light his fire, get him hot,
do everything that turns him on, except   840
the thing you're under oath not to. OK?

Myrrhine
Don't worry, I can do it.

Lysistrata
          Very well.
While you get ready I'll try to get *him* ready
and warm him up a bit. Now out of sight!

Rod
O woe is me! I've got a terrible cramp!   845
It's like I'm being broken on the rack!

Lysistrata
Who enters our defense perimeter?

---

838 In Greek the name is Kinesias of Paionidai, punning on *kinein* ('screw') and *paiein* ('bang').

Rod

     Me.

Lysistrata

 A man?

Rod

    Just look!

Lysistrata

      In that case please depart.

Rod

 Who's telling me to leave?

Lysistrata

        The daytime guard.

Rod

 I've come for Myrrhine. Tell her that I'm here!   850

Lysistrata

 You give me orders? Who do you think you are?

Rod

 Her husband, Rodney Balling, from Bangtown.

Lysistrata

 A lovely name! You know, we consider it
 our very favorite topic of conversation.
 Your wife has little else upon her lips.   855
 She'll eat bananas, or a peanut, sighing,
 'If only this were really Balling!'

Rod

       God!

Lysistrata

 Yes sir! And any time the conversation turns
 to men, your wife speaks up forthwith and says,
 'Compared to Balling, nothing else exists!'   860

Rod

 Please, call her out!

Lysistrata

     Got anything for me?

Rod

 Indeed I do. You're very welcome, too.
 What's mine is yours. How's this? It's what I've got.

Lysistrata

 I think I'll call your wife. Hold on.

Rod
Be quick!
I have no joy or pleasure in my life   865
since my Myrrhine up and left the house.
I open up the door and start to cry,
it looks so empty! Then I try to eat,
but I can hardly taste the food. I'm horny!

Myrrhine
I love him dearly, but he doesn't want   870
to love me back! Don't make me see him! Please!

Rod
Oh Pussikins, my darling, what's the matter?
Come down here!

Myrrhine
I'm not coming anywhere!

Rod
You won't obey me when I say to come?

Myrrhine
I fail to see a reason for your summons.   875

Rod
A reason? Don't you see what shape I'm in?

Myrrhine
Goodbye.

Rod
No, wait! Perhaps you'll want to hear
from Junior. Come on, yell for mommy, kid.

Baby
Mommy! Mommy! Mommy!

Rod
Well, what's the matter? Don't you pity him?   880
You know he's been six days without your breasts!

Myrrhine
I feel for Junior, but it's very clear
you don't.

Rod
Get down here, woman, and see your child!

Myrrhine
O motherhood, what a drag! I'll be right down.

Rod

She seems much sexier and even younger   885
than I remember. Very tasty looking!
She acted tough, and very haughty too,
but that just makes me want her even more!

Myrrhine

Poor sweetie pie! With such a lousy father.
I'll kiss and cuddle you, my darling child.   890

Rod

The hell you think you're doing, listening to
those women? You only piss me off and hurt
yourself as well.

Myrrhine

                    Don't lay your hands on me!

Rod

You know our home's an utter mess. You just
let everything go.

Myrrhine

                    It doesn't bother me.   895

Rod

It doesn't bother you that all your clothes
were dragged away by chickens?

Myrrhine

                                        Not at all.

Rod

And worse, your sacred duty as my mate
has been neglected! Thus you must return.

Myrrhine

I'm going nowhere till you swear on oath   900
to vote to end the war.

Rod

                                I'll maybe do that,
if it's appropriate.

Myrrhine

                        Then maybe I'll go home,
if it's appropriate. But now I'm sworn to stay.

Rod

OK, at least lie down with me awhile.

Myrrhine
I won't. But I don't say I wouldn't like to.   905

Rod
You would? Then why not do it, pussy mine?

Myrrhine
Oh really, Rod, in front of Junior here?

Rod
Of course not. Nurse, take Junior home at once.
All right, the kid's no longer in our way.
Let's do it!

Myrrhine
   Do it where, you silly man?   910
It's public here!

Rod
     You're right. Hey, there's a cave.

Myrrhine
I must be pure to re-enter the citadel.°

Rod
Then purify yourself in the sacred spring there.

Myrrhine
But what about my oath? I won't be perjured.

Rod
A women's oath means nothing. I'm not worried.   915

Myrrhine
Well, let me get a bed.

Rod
     But I don't need one:
the ground's OK by me.

Myrrhine
    I wouldn't dream
of making you lie there (though you deserve it).

Rod
She really loves me, that's quite obvious.

Myrrhine
Your bed, sir. Lie right down, I'll tuck you in.   920
But I forgot, what is it, yes, a mattress.

---

912 Sexual intercourse, like childbirth (742 n.), was forbidden in sanctuaries, and even wives
  who had not douched in running water after intercourse might pollute a sanctuary.

Rod

A mattress? None for me, thanks.

Myrrhine

                              I'm uncomfortable
on box-springs.

Rod

                    Give me just a little kiss?

Myrrhine

OK.

Rod

        Oh lordy! Get the mattress quick!

Myrrhine

And here it is. Stay down while I undress.   925
But I forget, what is it, yes, a pillow.

Rod

But I'm all set, I need no pillow.

Myrrhine

                              I do.

Rod

It's like a restaurant where they serve no food.°

Myrrhine

Lift up, now, up. Well, now I think I'm set.

Rod

I know I am! Come here to papa, darling!   930

Myrrhine

I'm taking off my bra. But don't forget,
don't lie to me about your vote for peace.

Rod

May lightning strike me!

Myrrhine

                              You don't have a blanket.

Rod

It's not a blanket I want! I want to get fucked!

Myrrhine

That's just what's going to happen. Back in a flash.   935

---

928 'This cock of mine is like Heracles cheated of his supper.' The he-man hero Heracles was
     portrayed in myths as having a giant appetite for food and sex and getting into many
     embarrassing situations as a result.

Rod
That woman drives me nuts with all her bedding.

Myrrhine
Get up now.

Rod
    But I've already got it up!

Myrrhine
You want some perfume?

Rod
       Thank you, no, I don't.

Myrrhine
But I do, if it's all the same to you.

Rod
Then get the goddamned perfume. Holy Zeus!   940

Myrrhine
Hold out your hand. And save a bit for me.

Rod
I don't like perfume as a general rule,
unless it smells like love is in the air.

Myrrhine
Oh silly me, I must have brought Brand X.°

Rod
No, wait, I like it!

Myrrhine
    You're just being polite.   945

Rod
God damn the guy who first invented perfume!

Myrrhine
I found some good stuff. Here's the tube.

Rod
       Here's mine!
Come on now, let's lie down, there's nothing more
to fetch.

Myrrhine
  You're right, I will, I'll be right there.
I'm taking off my shoes. Remember, dear,   950
your promise to vote for peace.

---

944 'Brand X': perfume from Rhodes, one of the allies that had defected after the Sicilian disaster and whose perfume may have been an inferior product.

Rod

I surely will.
Where are you? Hey Myrrhine! Where's my pussikins?
She pumped me up and dropped me flat. I'm ruined!

Duet

What'll I do? No one to screw!°
  I've lost the sexiest girl I knew.   955
My cock is an orphan,
  it couldn't be worse.
I'll just have to get him°
  a practical nurse.

Men's Leader

Frightful deceit! Pity on you!
We cannot imagine what to do.   960
What balls can endure
  being treated this way,   965
without any chance of
  an actual lay?

Rod

Oh god, the cramps attack anew!

Leader

A dirty bitch did this to you!

Rod

Oh no, she's really sweet and kind.   970

Leader

That bitch? You must have lost your mind!

Rod

You're right, a bitch
  is what she is!
I'll put a curse
  upon that miz!

I pray for a tornado,
  with lightning bolts and all,
to lift her into heaven
and then to let her fall.   975

Way down and down she's falling,
  above a giant rock.

---

954 This duet parodies the high pathos of tragic laments in its rhythm and music, but the
    obscene language and the ludicrous predicament lamented are purely comic.
957 See 725 n.

And when she's almost on it,
  I pray she hits my cock!

Spartan Herald

Direct me, please, to party headquarters. 980
Where are your commissars? You please will speak.

Rod

The hell are you? A man or a Freudian nightmare?°

Spartan Herald

I'm Herald from Sparta, you very cute young man.°
I come with orders to propose a treaty.

Rod

Then why have you got that tommy-gun in there? 985

Spartan Herald

Is not a weapon.

Rod

                    Turn around, let's see.
What's pushing out your trousers? What's in there,
your lunch-box?

Spartan Herald

                    This young man is obviously
intoxicated.

Rod

                    That's a hard-on, rogue!

Spartan Herald

Do not be silly, please: is no such thing. 990

Rod

Then what do you call that?

Spartan Herald

                    Is my attache case.°

Rod

If that's the case, then I've got one just like it.
But let's come clean, OK? I know what's up.
How fare you all in happy Sparta, sir?

Spartan Herald

Not well. The comrades rise, also the allies. 995

---

982 'or a Konisalos,' a phallic demon worshipped in Spartan territories.
982 According to Athenian humorists, Spartans were fond of anal intercourse with women
     and with adult men, both of which were distasteful to Athenians. Aristophanes keeps
     up this motif throughout the following scenes with Spartans.
991 'attache case': the Spartan 'dispatch-stick' (skytale), which was wrapped with leather
     strips containing coded messages and thus resembled the comic phallos.

We all have hard-on. Have a pussy shortage.

Rod

What's wrong? Some difficulty with your five
year plan?

Spartan Herald

   Oh no, was dissidents. Was Lampito.
She lead the women comrades in a plot.
They take an oath of solidarity,   1000
keep men away from warm and furry place.

Rod

What happened?

Spartan Herald

    Now we suffer! Walk around
like men with hernia problem,° all bent over.
The women won't permit to touch the pussy,
till each and every party member swear   1005
to make bilateral disarmament.

Rod

So this is global, a vast conspiracy
devised by women! Now I see it all!
Go quickly back to Sparta for the truce.
Arrange to send ambassadors with full powers. 1010
And I will so instruct our leaders here,
to name ambassadors. I'll show them this!°

Spartan Herald

I fly away. You offer good advice.

Choral Dialogue

Men's Leader

No animal exists more stubborn than a woman.
Not even fire, nor any panther, is quite as shameless. 1015

Women's Leader

You seem to understand this, but still you keep on fighting.
It's possible, bad man, to have our lasting friendship.

Men's Leader

 I'll never cease to loathe the female sex!

Women's Leader

That's up to you, I guess. But meanwhile I don't like
the sight of you undressed. Just look at you, how silly! 1020
I simply must come over and put your shirt back on.

1003 'like lampbearers,' who had to bend over to keep the wind from extinguishing the
   flame.
1012 'this': he flourishes his phallos.

Men's Leader
By god, I'd have to say that's no bad thing you did.
And now I'm sorry I took it off before, in anger.

Women's Leader
And now you look like a man again, and not so comic.
And if you hadn't been so hostile, I'd have removed   1025
that bug in your eye, which I can see is still in there.

Men's Leader
So that's what's been rubbing me the wrong way. Here's my ring.
Please dig it out of my eye, and then I want to see it.
By god, that thing's been biting at my eye a long time.

Women's Leader
You're very welcome. Stand still! What a grumpy man!   1030
Great gods, it's huge, a genuinely king-sized gnat.
And there it comes. Look at it. Isn't it Brobdingnagian?°

Men's Leader
You've helped me out a lot. That thing's been digging wells.
And now that it's removed, my eyes are streaming tears.

Women's Leader
There, there, you naughty man, I'll wipe your tears away,   1035
and kiss you.

Men's Leader
                    I don't want a kiss!

Women's Leader
                              I'll kiss you anyway!

Men's Leader
You got me, damn you. Women know how to get what they want.
That ancient adage puts it well and sums it up:
women are bad, you can't live with 'em, you can't live without 'em.
But now let's have a truce. We promise never again   1040
to flout you; and you promise never again to hit us.
So now let's get together and sing a happy song!

Chorus (8¹)
No citizen need fear from us°
    the slightest castigation.   1045

1032 'Trikorysian,' characteristic of a swampy region near Marathon (285 n.) where insects must have been large and numerous.

1045 At this point in a comedy the chorus, which has dropped the special identity it had during its active involvement in the plot, often sings free-form abusive songs about individual spectators. Here, in line with the play's theme of reconciliation, the chorus eschews such abuse. An additional reason may well have been Aristophanes' fear of ruffling too many feathers at an unusually tense time.

In recent times we've had our fill
  of trial and tribulation.

Instead , if any man and wife   1050
  should need some extra dough,
we'll gladly let you have what's in
  our piggy banks at home.

And when the war is over with,   1055
  don't bother to repay,
for what we have to loan you now
  is nothing anyway.

Chorus (8²)
Tomorrow night we'll have a feast,
  a real celebrity ball.   1060
We'll roast a pig and make some soup:
  we'll have enough for all.
So get up early, bathe the kids,
  and bathe yourselves as well.   1065
Then come on over, walk right in:
  you needn't ring the bell.

Then straight on to the dining room,
  as if it were your own.
We'll treat you just as you'd treat us: 1070
  there'll be nobody home.

SCENE V

Chorus Leader
Here they come, ambassadors from
  Sparta. Look, I see their beards.
What's around their waists? They might be
  wearing pig-pens under there.

Ambassadors from Sparta, first: our greetings.
Then tell us, please, what seems to be the matter?   1075

Spartan Ambassador
No use to waste a lot of time describing.
Is best to show condition we are in.

Leader
Oh my! Your problem's big and very hard.
It looks to me like runaway inflation.

Spartan Ambassador
> Unspeakable. What can one say? We wish   1080
> to talk of peace on any reasonable terms.

Leader
> And now I see our own ambassadors.
> They look like wrestlers hunkered down like that.
> Their pants appear to walk ahead of them.
> They suffer from a dislocated boner.   1085

Athenian Ambassador
> Can anyone direct me to Lysistrata?
> It's obvious we need to find her fast.

Leader
> Their syndrome seems to be the same as *theirs*.
> These spasms: are they worse in the wee hours?

Athenian Ambassador
> They're always bad and getting even badder!   1090
> Unless we get a treaty pretty quick,
> we'll have to start resorting to each other!°

Leader
> You'll cover up, if you've got any sense.
> Some fundamentalist° might chop it off.

Athenian Ambassador
> God, yes, good thinking.

Spartan Ambassador
>   Da, is very straight   1095
> advice. Come on, let's pull the trousers up.

Athenian Ambassador
> So: greetings, Spartans. Shameful situation!

1092 'resort to Cleisthenes,' who for some reason was perennially mocked by comic poets for submitting to anal penetration. Such a charge, if it could be established in the eyes of a jury, could result in the accused losing his citizen rights. Apparently no one had so accused Cleisthenes or been able to convince a jury, but there must have been gossip and comic poets evidently felt safe in exploiting it for this kind of off-hand mockery.

1094 'fundamentalist': 'one of the hermocopidae (Hermes-choppers), an allusion to a notorious incident that occurred just before the Sicilian Expedition sailed in 415. One morning, Athenians discovered that during the previous night the streetside statues of Hermes (patron god of travellers), a common sight all over Athens, had been vandalized by defacement. Some of the statues had phalloi and these had been knocked off. The authorities rounded up the 'usual suspects' (men known to have anti-democratic or anti-war sympathies), but the Athenians were never satisfied that all those responsible had been identified, and the whole incident remained a mystery. The bearded and ithyphallic men in our scene reminded Aristophanes of Hermes, and he insinuates that some of the 'choppers' may be among the spectators.

Spartan Ambassador

Da, comrade, terrible, but would be worse,
if decadent religious ones had seen us.

Athenian Ambassador

All right then, Spartans, time to play our cards.   1100
The reason for your visit?

Spartan Ambassador

                              Negotiation
for peace.

Athenian Ambassador

          That's very good. We want the same.
So now we've got to call Lysistrata,
for she alone can be our arbitrator.

Spartan Ambassador

Lysistratos, Lysistrata, whoever.   1105

Athenian Ambassador

It doesn't look as if we need to call her.
She must have heard us: here she comes herself.

Leader

Hail the bravest of all women!
  Now you must be more besides:
Firm but soft, high-class but low-brow,
  Strict but lenient, versatile.

Delegates from every city,
  captured by your potent charms,   1110
Come before you and request your
  arbitration of their cause.

Lysistrata

My task will not be difficult, since they're all
aroused and not at one another's throats.
How ripe are they? Where's Reconciliation?°
Take hold of the Spartans first, and bring them here.   1115
Be gentle with your hand and don't pull hard,
don't grab and yank the way men handle women,
but use a woman's touch, like home sweet home.
They won't extend a hand? Go farther down.

1114 Reconciliation is personified by a naked girl (that is, a male actor so costumed). She provides comic relief, in the form of lewd asides, during Lysistrata's earnest speeches and creates opportunity for by-play, being used as a map of Greece during the negotiations. Aristophanes typically portrays peace in terms of sensory enjoyments (food, drink, sex and festivals).

Now do the same for our Athenians.	1120
Whatever they extend, take hold of that.	
Now, men of Sparta, stand here on my left,	
and you stand on my right. Both parties listen.	
I'm female, yes, but still I've got a brain.	
I'm not so badly off for judgment, either.	1125
My father and some other elders, too,	
have given me a first-rate education.	
In no uncertain terms I must reproach you,°	
both sides, and rightly. Don't you share a cup	
at common altars, for common gods, like brothers,	1130
at the Olympic games, Thermophylai and Delphi?	
I needn't list the many, many others.	
The world is full of foreigners you could fight,	
but it's Greek men and cities you destroy!	
And that's the first reproach I have for you.	1135

Spartan Ambassador
My hard-on's absolutely killing me!

Lysistrata
Now, Spartans, my next reproach is aimed at you.
You must remember, not so long ago,°

1128 Lysistrata's arguments in the following speeches are, after we allow for comic exaggeration, essentially the ones that anti-war groups in fact advanced: let Greeks fight not Greeks but Asian foreigners, our traditional enemies; let us return to the pre-war arrangement, when Athens and Sparta enjoyed peaceful relations and joint hegemony in Greece, and when both gloriously resisted foreign interference in Europe; remember the mutual good deeds of the past. Comic poets, in the context of festive good feeling and nostalgia, could advance such appeals more easily than could politicians or generals.

Reference to 'foreigners' has an implication that would have made the Athenians feel self-righteous. The Spartans had, since the Sicilian disaster, been getting financial assistance from Persia. The Athenians, on the other hand, had for at least three years been supporting rebels against the Persian King. Aristophanes does not stress this potential slur against the Spartans because his main concern is to make an effective case for renewed peace with them. Only after this play was performed did Aristophanes and his audience learn that some of their own leaders had been negotiating secretly with the Persians for financial assistance.

1138 The great earthquake that devastated Sparta in 464 was followed by a revolt of Sparta's subject populations: helots (public slaves) and Messenians. The rebels fortified themselves on Mount Ithome, and the Spartans appealed for help from their allies, including Athens. The Athenians were divided: the radical democrats (the young Pericles among them) wanted to refuse the request, the conservative democrats wanted to honor it. The latter finally prevailed, sending their leader Cimon with a large army to Sparta. As a result of political infighting on both sides, the Spartans soon sent Cimon home in disgrace, and he was expelled from Athens the following year. This incident was a milestone in Athenian-Spartan enmity and strengthened anti-Spartan feeling at Athens. Here Lysistrata, with a good deal of rhetorical exaggeration, blames the 'Spartans' for starting the feud, but at the same time urges that the damage be put right by returning to the policy of Cimon.

you sent a man to Athens begging us,
on bended knee and whiter than a ghost,   1140
to send an army? All your slaves were up
in arms when that big earthquake hit you.
We sent you help, four thousand infantry,
a force that saved your entire country for you.
And now you pay the Athenians back by ravaging   1145
their country, after all they did for yours?

Athenian Ambassador
That's right, Lysistrata, they're in the wrong!

Spartan Ambassador
We're wrong: but take a look at that sweet ass!

Lysistrata
Do you Athenians think I'll let you off?
You must remember, not so long ago,°   1150
when you wore rags, oppressed by tyranny,
and Spartans routed the army of occupation,
destroying the tyrant's men and all his allies,
and drove them out on a single glorious day,
and set you free, and then replaced your rags   1155
with clothes befitting democratic people?

Spartan Ambassador
I never saw so well-endowed a woman!

Athenian Ambassador
I never saw a better-looking pussy!

1150 With parallel exaggeration (1138 n.), Lysistrata portrays the Athenian tyranny (concentration of power in one family through its alliances with other families) as a monstrously oppressive regime whose end was the beginning of the democracy: in this she caters to popular belief (274 n.). In reality, the period of tyranny in Athens was productive and prosperous and had proto-democratic features. Real democracy was not established upon the fall of the tyranny but only gradually in the course of the following half-century. The last Athenian tyrant was Hippias. After the assassination of his brother in 514 (633 n.), Hippias' rule became oppressive, and he had to exile many rivals for power, among them the Alcmaeonidae clan (maternal family of Pericles and Alcibiades, powerful advocates of the present war). The first attempt of the exiles to overthrow Hippias, at Leipsydrion (666 n.), was a failure, but by 510 the Spartans had come in on their side. In that year a Spartan land force under Cleomenes (see 274 n.) routed the Thessalian supporters of Hippias and besieged the tyrant's men on the Acropolis . After a two-day siege they escaped, never to return. A century later, opinions differed about who had had the most to do with liberation from Hippias' rule. Those who supported the war argued that it was the Alcmaeonidai; those who urged peace stressed the Spartan assistance.

Lysistrata
Considering all these mutual benefactions,
why prosecute the war and make more trouble? 1160
Why not make peace? What keeps you still apart?

Spartan Ambassador
We must demand this promontory here°
return to us.

Lysistrata
Which one?

Spartan Ambassador
This one in back:
we count on having, we can almost feel it.

Athenian Ambassador
By the God of Earthquakes, that you'll never get! 1165

Lysistrata
You'll give it up, sir.

Athenian Ambassador
What do *we* get, then?

Lysistrata
You'll ask for something that's of equal value.

Athenian Ambassador
Let's see now, I know, give us first of all
the furry triangle here, the gulf that runs
behind it, also the two connecting legs. 1170

Spartan Ambassador
My dear ambassador, you want it all!

Lysistrata
You'll give it. Don't be squabbling over legs.

Athenian Ambassador
I'm set to strip and do a little ploughing!

Spartan Ambassador
Me first: before one ploughs one spreads manure!

Lysistrata
When peace is made you'll both do all you want. 1175

1162 The places mentioned during the negotiations had actually been captured during the war and might have been mentioned were real negotiations held. But they were chosen primarily as having sexual double meanings that could be illustrated by reference to Reconciliation's naked body (1114 n.): Pylos ('gate' = anus); Echinous ('sea-urchin' = pubic hair); the Melian Gulf (vagina); the Megarian Walls (legs). According to stereotype, the Spartans like the rear end (982 n.) and the Athenians the other, so that the settlement is satisfactory.

For now, are each of these items to your liking?
If so you'd best confer with all your allies.

Athenian Ambassador

Confer with allies? Too hard up for that.
They'll go along with us. I'm sure they're just
as anxious to start fucking.

Spartan Ambassador

                  Also ours,   1180
is certain.

Athenian Ambassador

         Every Greek is fond of fucking.

Lysistrata

You argue well. And now for ratification.
The women on the citadel will host
the banquet, for we brought our picnic boxes.
You'll swear your oaths and make your pledges there.   1185
And then let everybody take his wife
and go on home.°

Athenian Ambassador

            What are we waiting for?

Spartan Ambassador

Please, lead the way.

Athenian Ambassador

            You'd best start running them!

Chorus (8³)

Fine gowns, embroidered shawls, kid gloves,
  and lots of golden rings: 1190
if you've a debutante at home,
  you needn't buy these things.

We've got a closet in the house,
  we've got a jewelry box.   1195
They're neither of them sealed so tight
  we couldn't pick the locks.

1186 Apparently Lysistrata's last words in the play: her plan has been a success and all that
remains of the plot is the celebration, which typically ends an Old Comedy, and the men's
promise to be better in the future. For these Lysistrata is not needed. In *Assemblywomen*,
Aristophanes similarly abandons a heroine when the plot no longer needs her. An early
disappearance of the main character, however, would violate a modern audience's sense
of theatrical symmetry. For possible solutions to this problem see 1273 n.

So come around, feel free to take
   whatever you can find. 1200
But you won't find much unless you have
   a sharper eye than mine.

Chorus (8⁴)

All those with many mouths to feed
   but nothing to provide:
we bought a peck of wheat and made 1205
   some bread to put aside.

So anyone who's poor can bring 1210
   a basket or a tray.
We've told our slaves to fetch the bread
   and give it all away.

One thing we should have told you first:
   you can't get near the door.
We've got a giant doberman
   who doesn't like the poor. 1215

SCENE VI

Athenian Ambassador

Open up the gate you!° Should have got out of my way!
You slaves, quit loafing. How'd you like your hair
burned off? Slave-beating: what a stale routine!
Director, I won't do it. Ask the audience?
All right, to please you I'll go through with it. 1220

Athenian

We're right behind you, glad to help you out.
Get lost, you slaves! Your hair's in serious danger!

Athenian Ambassador

Get lost: we'd like the Spartans to depart
from their banquet without stumbling over you.

Athenian

I've never seen a banquet quite like this. 1225
The Spartans were delightful company.
And we were pretty clever over drinks.

Athenian Ambassador

That's right. You can't be clever when you're sober.
I'm going to propose new legislation,

1216 A comic reversal of the previous action, when men tried to break into, not out of, the
   Acropolis .

that diplomats conduct their business drunk.	1230
As things now stand, we go to Sparta sober,	
then look for ways to stir up lots of trouble.	
And so whatever they say we never hear it,	
but hunt for hidden meaning in what they don't say,	
and then make contradictory reports.	1235
But now we're straightened out. If someone made	
a toast to workers rather than to profits,°	
we cheered him anyway and raised our glasses.	
What's this? Those slaves are coming back again.	
We told you: bugger off, you whipping posts!	1240

Athenian
That's right: the Spartans are emerging now.

Spartan Ambassador
Comrade musician, ready the Spartan bagpipes.
For now I dance and sing a happy song
to honor jointly both our superpowers.

Athenian Ambassador
A splendid treat: some genuine Spartan music!　　　　1245
I love to see you Spartans sing and dance.

Spartan Ambassador
Holy Memory, reveal°
　the glory days of yore:
how Spartans and Athenians　　　　　　　　　　　1250
　won the Persian war.

Athens met them on the sea,
　and Sparta held the land,
although the Persian forces were　　　　　　　　　　1260
　more numerous than sand.

All the gods that helped us then,°
　we bid you visit us again,
to help us celebrate our peace
　and see that it will never cease.　　　　　　　　　1265

1237 Choosing and singing the appropriate song at a banquet was an important social grace. At a diplomatic banquet the songs might have political significance: here the mood was so jovial that even provocative choices were not considered offensive.

1248 The Spartan Ambassador recollects two great battles of 480: the Athenian naval victory at Artemisium and the heroic stand of 300 Spartans under Leonidas against superior Persian forces at Thermopylae.

1262 He invokes Artemis Agrotera, worshiped both at Sparta and at Athens, where her birthday had come to commemorate the victory at Marathon (285 n.).

Now let mutual friendship reign,
  let's never fight a war again.
Put a stop to competition,
  end all mutual suspicion.   1270

Hear our prayer, gods, loud and clear.
  Witness what we promise here.

Athenian Ambassador
Well, now that everything has turned out well,°
reclaim your wives here, Spartans. These are yours,
Athenians. Every husband join his wife,   1275
and wife her husband. Then let's have a dance
and ask the gods to bless us, promising
never again to make the same mistakes.

Form up the dance, the Graces call,
summon Apollo, who heals us all,
Artemis his twin sister too,   1280
Bacchos with his maenad crew,
Father Zeus with lightning crowned,   1285
Hera, Zeus' wife renowned.
Summon every force above,
join us in our dance of love,
peace and freedom are at hand,
thanks to Aphrodite's plan!   1290

Chorus
What can we say?
horray, horray!
We also pray
you liked the play!

Athenian Ambassador
Hey Spartan, what about another song?   1295

Spartan Ambassador
To Sparta, Muse, my song will roam,
where Apollo has his southern home,
where Athena's house has brazen portals,
where Zeus' twin sons, knights immortal,   1300
gallop by Eurotas River,

1273 In the original performance, the Athenian Ambassador made this speech and sang the
  following song (to match his Spartan counterpart); meanwhile Lysistrata escorted the
  wives from the citadel and stood Athena-like in the gateway, above and behind the action. A modern director, however, may prefer to have Lysistrata take this part in order
  to involve the heroine more prominently in the finale.

setting Spartan hearts aquiver,
where heavenly dancers leap and shout,   1305
like colts the maidens frisk about,
raising dust, tossing their manes,   1310
possessed by Bacchus, all insane,
led by Zeus' holy child,
Helen, women's nonpareil.   1315

Hold your hair up with your hand,
beat your feet throughout the land,
help the dancers make some noise,
sing a song of joyous praise
for Athena of Athens, for Spartan Athena   1320
of the House of Bronze!